Kippenberger's Beer

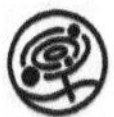

"I don't believe in art. I believe in artists."

— MARCEL DUCHAMP

1

Everyone suspected he was dead long before his body was recovered. Martin had been a legendary drunk, and many tall tales circulated around the New York art scene concerning his boorish excesses. For years, his close friends watched as he teetered on the edge, dipping his toe into the abyss that would destroy him. None of my associates were surprised when his body washed ashore. But Martin's bloated corpse didn't betray his alcoholic liver and innards. His cadaver looked like death was the ultimate hangover and bummer.

To be honest, I barely knew Martin, but I had considered him a friend since the moment we met. I first saw him in the spring of 1996, at an art opening one brisk night in Alphabet City, where a lot of art spaces had begun popping up around that time. It was one of those nights when winter's freezing winds seemed to be slowly dying down, but still weighed heavily in my bones and in the garbage-stinking air of the East Village.

I can't remember the artist's name who was showing that

night, but I do remember the show itself. It was too terrible to forget. The tiny, cramped storefront space was narrow and packed with a bohemian crowd of pierced faces with black puffy jackets, chunky sneakers and Doc Marten boots planted firmly on the grimy linoleum floor.

The artist's work was nothing more than fallen leaves gathered from the streets of New York, arranged in a grid along one wall, each placed with a thumb tack. The other wall displayed a series of "trash paintings." The artist had made them by dipping full bags of refuse from his studio into paint, and then dragging them over the canvas a few times. The results were less than spectacular. Calling them "trash paintings" was an understatement.

After standing as much as I could of the exhibition, I stepped out of the gallery into the leaves and trash on Avenue B and joined the crowd for a cigarette. I pulled my pack out of my trusty trench coat and took stock of the scene before me. I didn't recognize any of the people in the crowd. Typically, I saw a few familiar, friendly aesthetes at these types of shows, but not that night.

As I was planning to head home, I saw a dapper man in a black suit lurching down the street. Something about his presence radiated an intensity so palpable I could feel it from even several yards away. There was something different about him as he stumbled down the street. It wasn't just drunkenness that he exuded. I recognized him after a few seconds—it was Martin Kippenberger.

I'd long been fascinated by his reputation and his work, and I couldn't believe he was slumming it at a show like this. Martin was an enigmatic presence who would randomly show up every once in a while in the New York art scene. Some thought he was a chauvinist asshole, full of too much hubris and megalomania, a bloated relic of eighties yuppie-existentialism. He stood on tables and bars while he was wasted and sang dirty songs, his lyrics an affront to bourgeois notions of politically correct society. His jabs were legendary. People would mention he was in town and then recount his most recent diatribe against whoever was having a moment of success in the art scene.

I wondered what Martin would think of the work being passed off as art inside the gallery, and felt bad for what he was about to witness. I peeked through the window and watched as the crowd inside gathered around him. His magnetism had quickly pulled all the attendees into a state of devoted rapture. I lit another cigarette and waited to see if I'd have the chance to introduce myself.

I had a good excuse to try and befriend Martin: a solo show coming up in Cologne, with Martin's close friend and dealer there Christian Nagel. One of my goals for my trip to Cologne had been to meet Martin Kippenberger, as well as his infamous circle of friends. I had hoped it would happen sooner or later, and in that moment, at that shitty excuse for an art show, I felt fate smiling down on me from the heavens. Although I'd later find out that fate had nothing to do with it.

Martin burst out of the gallery and a throng of people followed him out onto the street. Everyone seemed drunk as shit, and I figured they were probably trying to find a place to keep the drinks flowing. With nothing better to do, I decided to tail them and eventually found myself part of the entourage. Nobody seemed to mind that I'd joined their revelry. They were probably too drunk to notice anyways.

Eventually, the crowd stuffed itself into a dive bar on Avenue C. A flickering neon sign that read "BEER" droned blue behind the bar while a Hank Williams song whimpered over the chatter of downtrodden barflies. I ordered a martini, trying my best to keep up with the voracious buzz emanating from

Martin and his crew.

I tried to make sense of the people surrounding him. Who were these drunk assholes? Some seemed to be very wealthy and were dressed in designer clothes that cost more than every painting I'd sold in my life combined. And then there were a few dirty-looking artist types such as myself. None of their faces registered in the rolodex of my memory. A couple sounded like Americans, but I also heard exotic accents—German, French, and Russian, I guessed. It was quite an international scene. The only unifying factor seemed to be a predilection toward alcoholism.

I stayed at the periphery, trying to not do anything that would cause anyone to question my presence amongst the group. I ordered another martini and sipped it at the bar. I zoned out a bit, hoping the drink would help me work up the nerve to talk to Martin.

An elbow bumped into my side. I was pissed that some drunken idiot had crashed into me, until I turned around and saw who the elbow belonged to. My eyes brightly opened as my lips parted with disbelief before turning into a grin.

"Hey! Who are you?" Martin Kippenberger asked as he sat down on the empty bar stool next to me.

I stuck out my hand to shake his hand. "I'm Johnny Dabs," I said, smiling wide as Martin took my hand. The whites of Martin's eyes were glazed pink, and he smelled like a pungent mixture of alcohol and sweat.

"Here," he said, reaching into his coat pocket and pulling out a flask. He passed it to me and motioned with his hands for me to drink up—or at least that's the message I imagined his drunken contortions were supposed to convey.

I took a sip and the harshest hooch I'd ever tasted roared down my now-burning throat. I felt my mouth go numb as though I was being prepared for dental surgery. My face burned like hot coal. My vision instantly softened and everything in the room moved at a slower pace. I looked down into my martini glass as it began to vibrate with an intensity I hadn't recognized before. "Jesus fucking Christ! That's some strong shit!" I said in between involuntary retches. I took a moment to compose myself. "You're Martin Kippenberger, right?"

"Ah, my reputation precedes me," he said. "You must be an artist. I can smell it on you. Or are you a hard-boiled dick?" Martin pointed at the khaki trench coat I was wearing and laughed.

I'd taken to wearing trench coats a few years ago, hoping to look like a mysterious character from a film noir, and had even grown a mustache to complete the picture. Haberdashery wasn't my thing, so I never wore a hat. I hoped I looked full of intrigue, but mainly thought I looked like a gay cop. But that was cool with me too.

"Yeah, I'm an artist," I said, happy Martin had blown my cover. "Actually, I have a show in Cologne coming up with your friend Christian Nagel. I was hoping to meet you when I was out there, but it's nice to meet you here in the city."

"You know Christian?" Kippenberger's eyes widened. "When's your show? I don't live there anymore, but I'm there often."

This was going better than I could have hoped. "It's in about two months." I said. My face burned red with a mixture of pride and embarrassment that I would be showing my work at the same gallery as the legend seated next to me.

"Is your studio around here?" Martin asked.

I told Martin my studio was a twenty-minute walk away, and he took another hit of the hooch.

"Well, let's go!" Martin said, passing the flask back to me. "I want to see your work."

I took a drink and winced before following Martin out of the bar.

I'd heard Martin had a reputation for supporting his friends, buying their work, putting it in his own shows, and wheeling and dealing on their behalf, but I still couldn't believe my luck.

We drunkenly walked along the edge of Tompkins Square Park, observing the down-and-out junkies of that mad city. Martin was obviously drunk, but somehow kept his wits in tact. He wasn't sloppy. I wondered if he was stoned as well, but he didn't give off the vibe of a stoner. It seemed like he was in his own world, taking in every detail of the city, lost in contemplation of a reality that I couldn't perceive. An eerie sensation flooded my body. Things appeared to percolate with a potency that began to frighten me, and I couldn't place why I was feeling this way. I thought it might've just been the effects of whatever was in Martin's flask. I was definitely more drunk than usual and my body felt weightless and airy as I tried to keep up with Martin's exuberant rambling. A gust of cold wind blew, and I looked up at the trees in the park swaying in the breeze. The leafless branches appeared to be thousands of tiny hands reaching out to the world, trying to grasp the chilly air. A bum emerged from the park, pulling up his pants like he'd just finished taking a shit. He turned toward us, his eyes shining brightly in the dark before seeming to fall from his face. I quickly shook my head in disbelief, as the bum's eyeballs floated back into place. He began screaming gibberish, and walked in the opposite direction.

"Do you make big paintings?" Martin asked, ignoring the bum.

"Yeah, some of them are pretty big," I said.

"Good," Martin said. "Big paintings equal big money."

We found our way to the Bowery, passing Martin's flask back and forth as we walked to my studio on Great Jones Street. Martin seemed to be floating across the sidewalk, skipping and dancing on air, indifferent to the barrage of pedestrians and tourists around us. Meanwhile, I felt like my feet were sinking into the ground with every step. Everything around us seemed to glow and sparkle. I was seeing some weird shit and wasn't sure what was going on, but I did my best to keep my cool. I had Martin Kippenberger ready for a studio visit, and I didn't want to fuck anything up. When we reached my front door, I took another sip from Martin's flask. I wasn't sure what I was drinking, but whatever it was, it was strong.

In my loft, as Martin looked at my work, his whole demeanor changed. He was no longer gregarious and charming. Instead, he was mostly silent, only muttering to himself every few minutes in German. He paced around the studio, moving paintings back and forth around the room. He stopped at one and started laughing. He turned around, picked up a stack of drawings from a table, and rifled through them, tossing them back onto the table with indifference. He let out a sigh as he finished.

I took a seat in my fake Eames armchair and watched Martin survey my last few months of relentless painting. It seemed like he was trying to find the words to articulate his disappointment and boredom. Eventually, he sat down on the couch across from me.

"I see why Christian was drawn to your work," he finally slurred. "Your paintings look German. Are you German?"

"Uh, no, I, uh, I'm not German," I stuttered, feeling deflated. Strange shapes swirled around the room as a vibrant electricity pumped through the lights of my studio. My work seemed to pulse with defeat. Why was I seeing all this strange shit? I felt like I was about to get the spins, but I also felt surprisingly calm. Kippenberger's flask had fucked me up.

"You obviously like me and my friends' work," Martin said. "These look like something I would have seen in Cologne in 1985."

I knew it wasn't a compliment.

"You like Rodney Dangerfield?" Martin asked.

"The comedian? I guess he's pretty funny."

"I love his work," Martin said. Obviously he was beyond drunk if he was thinking of Rodney Dangerfield while looking at my paintings. "Can you imagine Robert Redford doing Rodney Dangerfield's material? Do you think it would be as funny?" It was a dumb question, but Martin seemed dead serious.

"I guess it wouldn't be as funny," I said, trying to figure out where he was steering the conversation.

"Well, then," he began. "Why would an American trying to make silly German paintings be funny at all? You're trying to be funny. You're trying to be smart. You're trying to be German. It doesn't work."

Martin proceeded to tell me my work lacked a German sensibility, and that collectors in Cologne would be thrown off by my futile attempts at humor. He asked if I was familiar with *Texte zur Kunst*, a German art journal that was setting the tone for a new climate in the Cologne scene. Everything they represented was much more heady, heavy, academic, theoretical, political, and politically correct than the work that had come out of Cologne in the eighties. It was a shift I'd seen supported by galleries in New York. Basically, they represented and championed everything my work wasn't.

It wasn't the booming eighties anymore. Galleries back then took lots of chances on young, emerging artists. But now, in 1996, galleries were closing all over the city, and getting your foot in the door at a decent gallery had about as much of a chance of happening as getting struck by lightning. The art market was slowing down, tightening its belt, waiting for the next wave of cash to flood the market with wet paintings ready to be flipped at auction a year after they were bought.

When the sun began to rise outside the windows of my loft, Martin finally got ready to leave. I stumbled to my door to say goodbye, feeling conflicted about what had happened. On one hand, I had just spent an evening in my loft with one of my favorite artists. On the other, he seemed to think my work was total shit. I thought he might be right.

I opened the window to smoke a cigarette and watched Martin walk down Great Jones towards the Bowery. Morning had erased the night, and the cold wind was still rushing through the streets and avenues. As Martin reached the corner, I saw two toughs in black overcoats emerge from a doorway. They were screaming something at Martin in a language I couldn't understand. A black Mercedes sped down the street and came to a full stop next to the commotion. I looked down at the trouble unfolding before me and felt an icy tingling in my spine, a warning of impending doom. The two men grabbed Martin by his arms and dragged him into the idling car. I knew there wasn't time for me to intervene. By the time I got out of my loft and down the street, they'd be gone. Besides, I was still properly wasted off of whatever had been in Martin's flask.

Taking a nervous drag from my cigarette, I watched as the car sped off with Martin Kippenberger in tow.

2

I spent the next few weeks preparing my work to be shipped off to Cologne, but I couldn't shake the scene I had witnessed after my first encounter with Martin. What had happened to him? What was that scuffle about? And who were those men? I was hoping to see Martin in Cologne so I could ask him about the incident.

In Cologne, as I walked from my hotel to Christian's gallery, a new uneasiness overtook my obsessive thoughts about Martin. I was overwhelmed and nervous about every aspect of my show. I had never been abroad before, and felt like a hayseed in the old metropolis. The beautiful city had Roman ruins next to modern buildings, ancient churches next to sleek, postmodern offices, homes, and retail spaces. The current era's penchant for minimalism stood out against the more ornate architecture from centuries ago. The art scene in Cologne was incredibly exciting in the eighties, and many great artists had come out of it. Since then, things had died down in Cologne, and Berlin had become the de facto cultural hub of Germany in the nineties.

On my first morning in Cologne, I sat down with Christian Nagel at Cafe Central, a breakfast buffet where many local artists hung out. I immediately noticed a group of twelve Martin Kippenberger paintings hung in a grid on the wall, and jumped out of my chair to get a closer look. It was probably rude to stand so close to a man and woman enjoying their breakfast in front of the paintings, but I didn't care. The paintings were too great for me to give a shit.

They were hung as if the twelve separate pieces were one large piece. The colors in all of the paintings were bright and loud and a few depicted political celebrities I recognized: a cartoonish caricature of Richard Nixon in the top left, looking smug and stupid; an impasto portrait of Ronald Reagan one painting over; a loose portrait of Yasser Arafat in the bottom right corner. I think one on the bottom row was of the philosopher Martin Heidegger, but I wasn't sure. Some of the others appeared to be more abstract portraits, but I didn't know who the subjects were and guessed they were European political figures I wasn't familiar with. It didn't matter to me who they were. It was a great Kippenberger painting regardless of my ignorance.

It didn't end there. As my new dealer took me out to lunches and dinners throughout the time we were setting up for the show, every restaurant and bar seemed to have at least one of Martin's works on the wall, along with pieces by other Cologne artists like Walter Dahn, Albert Oehlen, Rosemarie Trockel, Franz West, and others. Every piece I encountered of Martin's mesmerized me. I had already been a huge fan of his work, but by the end of my installation, my fandom had grown exponentially—I'd become a huge fanboy. I did my best to hide my obsession from Christian, trying to play it cool, but even in the least impressive restaurants, the paintings I saw were masterpieces. I couldn't help but squeal with delight at every new discovery of Martin's work. Christian eventually just rolled his eyes, and explained that Martin was often out of money, so he bartered his work to cover his exorbitant drink tabs.

The morning before my opening, as I was drying off after a shower, I heard a loud knock at my door. I wrapped a towel around my wet body, and opened the door. There was Martin Kippenberger standing before me, clutching a bottle of champagne.

"Johnny!" Martin said, as he pushed his way into the hotel room to give me a hug.

"Holy shit, man" I said. "It's great to see you. I was hoping I'd run into you while I was here."

Martin reeked of booze, and I got the feeling he probably hadn't slept a wink the night before. His face was haggard and disheveled, and the bags under his eyes looked like they held ten-ton weights. Both the whites of his eyes and his skin looked yellow and sickly, but the booze that was surely still in his system seemed to be keeping his spirits up.

Martin left to get some orange juice from the lobby to make mimosas, and I quickly got dressed. When he returned, we popped the bottle of champagne with a celebratory fervor even though it was only nine in the morning. After I poured myself a glass, Martin grabbed the bottle from me and drank the rest down in a few sloppy gulps.

"You got anymore of that moonshine we drank in New York?" I asked.

"God, no, not here," he said. "I can only get that in New York. If I had that stuff here I'd be dead. It's not for the weak of liver, as you might remember."

"Yeah," I said. "I haven't been that fucked up since I was a teenager. I also wanted to ask you . . . I saw you get thrown into a car after you left my loft. What was that all about?"

"Oh, that," he said, pausing as he stared off into the distance and rubbed his hands together, deep in thought. "Those were just some pushy collectors I know. They were hounding me for a studio visit the whole time I was in New York. I ran into them as I was heading back to my studio from your place. They wanted to see some new work, so they gave me a lift back to my studio. Nothing to worry about, except they didn't buy shit."

He seemed unperturbed by the event. He was convincing, but I still had a hard time believing him. Those men didn't look like typical collectors. They looked like violent criminals. And why would any collectors with enough money to buy Martin's work rough him up like that?

"Let's get out of here," Martin said, standing up. "I'll take you around the city."

We spent the day making stops at numerous little cafes and bars to keep our drunk steady. I was enamored with the tall and thin Kölsch beers we drank like water. Since I was a novice in the beginning phase of my art star lifestyle, every local ritual was imbued with significance. I was tickled as each little beer we drank was immediately refilled. Martin told me it was the custom, and to put my coaster over the beer to stop the bartenders from refilling my glass. I just let them keep coming instead, trying my best to keep up with Martin.

Martin walked at a hurried pace with an unceasing joie de vivre as we traveled from Cafe Central to the Broadway. I was beginning to feel a bit sleepy from all the beer, but Martin jumped onto the bar and began singing some sort of mangled version of a Rolling Stones song and doing his best Mick Jagger moves across the bar, causing a few glasses of beer to crash onto the floor in the process. It seemed obvious, even to someone as toasted as me, that not everyone was as enthusiastic about Martin's ridiculous performance as I was. Patrons gave him the stink eye, obviously not amused by his antics.

As we continued walking through the center of Cologne, I got the feeling we were being followed. I thought I kept seeing the same three men tailing us. I wasn't sure but the same faces seemed to appear everywhere we went, from Cafe Central to the Broadway, to our aimless meandering through the city. I realized I was feeling pretty drunk, disoriented and jet-lagged. My paranoia was intensified by how unfamiliar the city felt, but I was too blasted and exhausted to really give a shit. Besides, Martin was hilarious, and I decided to try to enjoy the time I had with one of my favorite artists.

Next we went to Gisela Capitain Gallery so Martin could stop in and say hello to Gisela and the rest of the staff, and then headed to the legendary Koenig Books. I browsed while Martin talked to the owner in the back room. Martin was restless everywhere we went, not wanting to linger anywhere for long. It was like following a tornado, watching it wreak havoc on Cologne.

After our stop at Koenig Books, Martin asked if there was anything I wanted to see in Cologne. I knew I wanted to check out the Museum Ludwig because I had read it had an impressive modern and contemporary collection, but Martin seemed uninterested by my request. He sighed as we approached the back entrance to the museum.

"I'm not going in," Martin said. "But feel free. Help yourself to the chocolate factory mausoleum."

I was confused, but said ok, and headed in alone.

I immediately walked toward a Niki de Saint-Phalle sculpture, feeling small next to the Venus of Willendorf-shaped woman, a red heart in place of her vagina. She looked like she'd been frozen in the middle of a dance after taking a tab of LSD. I continued to wander around, trying my best to take in the work in front of me, but I couldn't enjoy anything. I knew Martin Kippenberger was outside, bored out of his mind. I figured I should race through, see as much as I could in a timely fashion, but it was an impossible task. There were too many important pieces from art history on display. I rushed past a group of Otto Dix portraits, hurried by Ernst Ludwig Kirchner's famous portrait of the Die Brücke artists, caught a glimpse of a stunning Asger Jorn painting, and spent a few seconds standing in front of a Richard Lindner painting I'd never seen before. But even when standing in front of works by artists I idolized, I could only picture Martin standing outside by the water fountain, waiting for me to return. After all, Martin could be the Bridge leading me to grander pastures: a life of jet-setting, never-ending art sales, or simply joy itself as I imagined it. I tore myself away from each painting I tried to savor, feeling distress in every cell in my body. I still regret not spending more time there, but I couldn't leave Martin. I couldn't fuck up any chance to hang out with him. I guessed he meant just as much to me as all the masterpieces in the museum.

I headed out the door scanning the crowd outside for Martin. When I finally spotted him, I realized there were two men speaking with him. They were both very tall and imposing, but wore matching black Adidas tracksuits, maroon leather jackets, and black leather shoes, as if they were wearing a uniform. One had long, black hair and a long, black beard and looked like Rasputin. The other had close cropped hair on the crown of his head with longer bangs slicked down with hair gel. I immediately noticed a thick gold bracelet dangling from his wrist. The tops of his hands were covered in tattoos. As I walked closer, I could hear that their voices were raised. They were speaking in German, a language that had always sounded harsh to me. I couldn't understand what they were saying, but every word sounded like a threat. I couldn't be sure, but I got the feeling they weren't German. They looked out of place, out of sync with the German demeanor as I understood it. I couldn't imagine the men drinking Kölsch beers in any of the places we drank at earlier. They would've stuck out like a stinky pinky.

Martin turned towards me as I approached, and wrinkled his mouth into a smirk, before returning his attention to the men confronting him. I stood back and nervously grabbed a cigarette from my trench coat, hoping the situation would come to a peaceful end. I watched silently as Martin continued to speak to the men in German. I couldn't stop staring at the tattooed hands, as Martin motioned toward me and the two men looked in my direction with intimidating scowls. I was scared shitless. Then the men shook hands with Martin, seemingly wrapping up their conversation, and walked away and up the marble steps.

"What was that about?" I asked when the men were out of sight.

"Oh, nothing. Just some Russian collectors I know. I told them about your show."

"Those were collectors?" I asked. I knew I didn't want to see the likes of them at my opening.

"Did you enjoy the mausoleum?" Martin asked, ignoring my question. "I think I can smell the death on you."

He grabbed me by the shoulder, and led me off to more bars and more drinking, but I couldn't get the scene out of my mind. The intimidating men, the strange encounter, my day drunkenness, it all added a weight of dread to the rest of the day. As we drank more beers at a bar, I had difficulty believing the men were just Russian collectors. The Rasputin-looking motherfucker and the man with tattooed hands kept popping back into my thoughts. There was something fishy about them. And, it made me question Martin's story about getting thrown in the car outside my loft by some collectors. Who the fuck were these people collecting Martin's work?

We ate some pasta at one of Martin's favorite Italian spots, Ezios. Martin ordered the most expensive food and wine from the menu, but I never saw him pay for a thing. Of course, his work was on the walls of the establishment.

As it got late, Martin walked me back to my hotel. His assistant was waiting for him, idling in a car with the heater blasting. He gave me a hug, the smell of beer heavy on his breath, as well as his whole body. He told me to wait a second, ran to the back of the car, popped the trunk, and presented me with a stack of his books.

"For you, Johnny," he said, as he handed me the stack.

"Whoa," I said. "Thanks so much, and thanks for showing me around today."

"No problem," Martin said.

He got into the passenger seat of the car. The engine revved, and they sped away. A black Mercedes sedan with heavily tinted windows that was parked next to them started its engine, and then took off in a fury. I watched as it raced off, seemingly in pursuit of Martin. Were they following him? I felt too drunk to give it much thought and stumbled back to my room, not looking forward to the hangover that was sure to roar in my head all day before my opening.

The next day was my show's opening, and Christian passed on the news that the whole show had been bought sight unseen by a well-known German family of collectors. Apparently, they were huge patrons of Martin and a few of his contemporaries in the Cologne scene as well.

Martin showed up to the gallery and made it clear that he had been the one to orchestrate the sale of my show. At first he seemed genial, but as the night went on, I sensed he was jealous that the attention was on me, despite his attempts to make it otherwise. He began to act out, jumping on a table, trying to lead all the attendees in one of his sing-alongs to an old German folk song about a glow worm or something. He had about a dozen admirers that held onto his every word. The other thirty or so people at the opening just seemed annoyed.

After the song ended, Martin grabbed a bottle of champagne from the back of the gallery, popped the cork, and poured the cold champagne all over my head. He then gave a toast to me and Christian. I was pretty pissed, the champagne washing away my excitement and leaving me drenched in sticky wine. After the toast, Martin invited me to join him and his admirers at the next club to drink our livers pickled, but I was too hungover to try to keep up with his drinking habits. I was also angered by Martin's champagne stunt. It was such a dickhead move on his part. I decided to spend the rest of the night at Christian's house drinking wine, checking out his art collection, and trying to get a feel for whether he wanted to keep working with me. As the champagne on my clothes dried, I felt sticky but still elated by my successful show.

I departed the next day for New York, feeling hopeful and rejuvenated, but still hungover from it all. On my way back over the Atlantic, I thought about my time with Martin. Who were all these nefarious collectors surrounding him? If my career kept rising to the top, then would I also have to deal with a bunch of these frightening assholes?

3

Around this time, there was a lot of talk amongst my friends that everything was dead. Art was dead. Painting was dead. SoHo was dead. God was dead. Nietzsche was dead. Poetry was dead. The novel was dead. Cinema was dead. And, inevitably, New York was dead.

Many of my friends in New York had begun to look at the burgeoning art scene in Los Angeles with jealousy. There was definitely magic happening there, but I could never get behind the idea that New York wasn't the most important place to work as an artist. Sure, artists like Laura Owens, Mike Kelley, Monique Prieto, Paul McCarthy, and plenty more were making amazing work on the West Coast, but there were just as many exciting artists cranking out work in New York. To me, New York was where artists' dreams came true. Los Angeles? That was just Hollywood, the locus of filmmaking and celebrity, and would always be the place where actors', directors', and producers' dreams came true. Everything in Los Angeles revolved around Hollywood, and nothing, not even the art world, was immune to this fact.

Nonetheless, I wanted in on the West Coast action as well.

I had met Patrick, an art dealer from the City of Angels, about a month after I got back from Cologne, at a bar after an opening. There was a greasy air about him but he liked my work, and my friend Elena had shown with him a few months prior. She had good things to say about him. Or, at least her bank account did. She also got cringy vibes from him, but told me he sold everything she sent with speed and ease. Patrick urged me to send him some work for a group show he was putting on in Chinatown. Despite my reservations, I sent him a few paintings, hoping to keep pumping money into my wallet.

Not long after I sent the work, I arrived in Los Angeles to check out the group show Patrick put me in, and see if I could sell some paintings. I rented a car since I figured it was the only practical way to get around the sprawling megalopolis. I'd reserved a cheap economy car, but the only thing they had on the lot was a brand-new white Mustang convertible. It wasn't my style, but it had a CD player—a luxury at the time. I had brought one CD with me to listen to on my Walkman as I flew to Los Angeles: an album of madrigals by the sixteenth century composer Carlo Gesualdo.

I had first read about Gesualdo in a short story by Julio Cortázar. A few years before this trip—probably 1993—I was browsing at the Strand bookstore, looking at the used books in the fluorescent lit, dumpy basement, and found a first edition of Cortázar's collection of short stories called *We Love Glenda So Much*. The illustration on the cover looked like one of my paintings—a creamy white background, simplified faces, three mouths, three noses. but only four eyes—the middle face sharing its eyes with the faces on either side. I took it to Washington Square Park and read the story that would haunt me for years to

come: the story of a group of Latin American expatriates per-
forming the works of Gesualdo, finding themselves re-enacting
scenes from his life within their own claustrophobic world of
touring as a group, and singing Gesualdo's compositions for
appreciative audiences throughout the world.

I loved the way Gesualdo's madrigals sounded like a choir
of demented angels singing together, but there was also an evil
deed that added to the music's mystique. Gesualdo was just as
famous for having murdered his first wife and her lover after
catching them in bed post coitus as he was for his musical compositions. He mutilated both of their corpses, stringing their
entrails up for all the town to see. Because he was an Italian
count, part of the royal family, he was protected from prosecu-
tion. But that didn't stop his murdered wife's family from trying
to track him down. Gesualdo spent the rest of his life moving
from castle to castle, trying to evade the rage of his dead wife's
family while writing his strange musical compositions.

After I finished reading the Cortázar story, I had a hard time
tracking down an album of his songs. Eventually I found a
shop that exclusively sold classical music in Greenwich Village
called the Chopin Block. They had one soiled-looking CD
buried in the back, which the owner dug out for me before eyeing me suspiciously as he rang me up. I also went to the music
division of the New York Public Library many times, searching
for more information on Gesualdo, but it was difficult to find
many details about the infamous composer. The harder it was
to find information on Gesualdo, the more obsessed I became
with him. I felt like a detective from a mystery novel trying to
unearth the secret clue to unravel the mystery of Gesualdo's
terrible deeds. He was an abominable person—a murderer—
but holy shit, his madrigals took me to another eerie universe.
One day, I finally found a reproduction of a portrait of him in
an old book at the library, and made a photocopy of the por-

trait. I tacked up the portrait by my bed and hoped Gesualdo's ghost would protect me from harm. In hindsight, it didn't work so well.

And so I drove around L.A. with the Mustang's top down, the sun blistering my body, as I listened to the otherworldly sounds of this deranged man. The succulent gardens drooping off hills and cliffs, the calm blue of the ocean, the mountain views to the east, and the almost unnatural green of the vegetation as sunlight burned through the smog every morning—all of this gloriousness was magnified by the creepy voices harmoniously blaring from my CD player.

I wasn't just in LA to scope out the scene and sell some paintings like the traveling salesman I'd become. I also wanted to see my favorite painting in person, James Ensor's "Christ's Entry into Brussels." Since the Getty was in the process of building a billion-dollar museum center to house its collection, the painting was currently in storage at the opulent Getty Villa. Fortunately, my friend Elena knew a conservator at the Getty, and I'd been able to work out an appointment to see the painting.

On the day of my appointment, I cruised out to Pacific Palisades with the top down, blasting Gesualdo as I baked in traffic. I met my contact, and was granted exclusive access to the painting. She gave me a tour of the grounds as we walked to the room "Christ's Entry into Brussels" was stored in. The Villa itself was considered "a country home," but was more like a palace, complete with Greek and Roman antiquities everywhere, flowing fountains and pools, perfectly manicured lawns, flawlessly trimmed bushes and trees, gardens of unimaginable earthly delights, and, of course, a view from on high of the Pacific Ocean just beyond the P.C.H.

She took me to a huge, bright white room with rows of painting storage racks along the back wall, and the painting hung alone on a pristine white wall opposite, looking like a sleek gallery space tucked away in the conservatively decorated villa.

"You mind if I listen to some music on my headphones while I take this all in?" I asked her, as we stood before the massive painting.

"Sure," she said. "Just don't touch the painting or get too close. You've got half an hour before I have to escort you off the premises."

I pressed play and let the voices in my ears mingle with the faces in the crowd as I took in the epic scale of the painting. Art rarely had much of a physical impact on me, but a few paintings have given me goosebumps. I stared at all of the faces, all of the masks, all the hundreds of cartoony caricatures of the people of Brussels, the massive crowd of souls painted in bright, vivid colors, the thick globs of oil paint daubed into the likeness of joyous beings, the grotesque comedy of being a human in this world, the banner across the top that read: "VIVE LA SOCIALE," a visionary spectacle of modernity ambling through the streets—and all of the hairs on my arms, legs, and neck stood erect in recognition of the painting before me.

As I stood in front of the painting, I imagined all the painted caricatures as artists. Jesus was a background figure in the procession of people in jubilee, but was still the savior we all hoped for: the dealer who'd save us from poverty, the collector with a never-ending checkbook, infinitely funding an artist's creative pursuits. But in Ensor's composition, Jesus was almost hidden in the background, his halo a barely recognizable feature. I felt a tap on my shoulder, and turned to face the conservator.

"Time's up," she said.

It was still early afternoon, so I drove to Chinatown to see the group show I was in, and to see what was happening at the galleries there. I really dug the little pagodas, the dragons arching over the streets, and the red lamps hung throughout the squares. The shows looked like any other show I'd see in the East Village, just with brighter colors, more beachy breezes combing through the brush strokes, and less black. But after seeing my favorite painting, nothing could compare.

I met with Patrick and saw the group show. He told me he set up a lunch date in Venice the next day with some collectors that were interested in my work. I told him I'd be there.

The next day, I headed to a vegetarian restaurant in Venice to meet with Patrick and the collectors he'd mentioned the day before. The restaurant was voguish and sleek. Every surface was made out of concrete: the walls, the floors, the tables, the chairs. It wouldn't have surprised me if the food was made of concrete too. The waitstaff were all stunning, hopeful thespians and models, or whatever it was that pretty people did out here to become rich and famous. I could smell the salty ocean in the breeze, and watched as all the freaks streamed by on the boardwalk.

Patrick arrived with two potential collectors—neither of whom didn't seem excited to meet me or very interested in my presence whatsoever—as well as a vaguely European-looking man named Jacques, who Patrick introduced to me as his friend. As I shook Jacques's hand, I had the feeling I knew him from somewhere. And then it hit me—Jacques was a spitting image of the portrait of Gesualdo I had tacked up next to my bed, except with glistening, curly black hair slicked back. While he looked just like Gesualdo, he was dressed like an extra from a seventies B-movie in a green velvet suit, aviator sunglasses, and blue velvet loafers. He said he wasn't an artist, dealer, or collector, but he seemed to know everyone in the art world.

Finally I asked him, "Are you Italian?"

He laughed. "No, I'm Russian. You know Martin Kippenberger, right?"

He proceeded to tell me, and the rest of these Los Angeles art lovers, that Martin was talking about my show in Cologne, how he orchestrated the sale of it all. I tried my best to change the topic, knowing the gossip might alienate the collectors I was attempting to woo. I had been hoping they would want to buy some of my paintings, and from my experience, these types of people were usually pretty flighty. But, I knew the collectors weren't actually interested in buying my work. They ignored me for the most part, and didn't ask me a single question about me or my work.

Throughout the rest of the lunch, Jacques seemed to be watching my every move. I could feel his eyes burning my skin with their ceaseless stare, as champagne and wine flowed endlessly during the meal. In between talking loudly on their giant cellular phones, the rich collectors talked about the wine and their fine vintage as each bottle was brought out, but all of it was over my sauced head.

As what I hoped was the last bottle was being opened, I felt a tap on my knee under the table, and realized I'd drifted off into drunken day dreams of these collectors buying all my work, flying to some other major art world capital to sell more work to other disinterested collectors, repeating this process ad infinitum, while ignoring the chatter of these tedious blue bloods.

"Psst. Hey, Johnny," Jacques said across the table. "Try some of this."

I felt the tapping again, and realized Jacques was attempting to pass something to me under the table. Patrick and the collectors were lost in some argument about the best place to vacation in the South of France. I reached down, felt a flask in my hand, and brought it up to my mouth.

I took a swig, coughed, and almost spit out the booze. Instantly, I recognized the fiery rotgut of Martin's mysterious elixir. After just a sip, my vision had gone hazy, and I could feel my body turning into a puddle on the cool concrete seat.

"Did you get this from Martin?" I asked, my head swimming in the booze's magic.

"No," Jacques said, as he winked. "He got it from me. Are you going to Dmitry Vaga's party tonight?"

I told Jacques I hadn't known about the party, but I was curious. I kept hearing about Dmitry Vaga, a young art star who was supposedly the king of the L.A. scene. I figured it was time to actually see who this kid was.

"Say you know me," Jacques said, "and getting in won't be a problem."

From what I'd heard, Dmitry Vaga was one of the most successful young artists in Los Angeles. His raves were as legendary for their raucousness as for the cosmopolitan elites and celebrities that frequented them. Apparently, he was the scion of a notorious Russian family that somehow ended up in Los Angeles in the 1950s. They were Russian oligarchs, forced out of their homeland for some political reason or other. His father operated a global hedge fund worth a couple hundred million dollars. That grew their massive family wealth into even more money—money that now went into funding Dmitry's art career and parties.

I drove south of downtown LA to Boyle Heights, parked my car on the street, and got my first glimpse of Dmitry's massive studio complex. There were five warehouse buildings, each about five to ten thousand square feet in an old and seemingly forgotten warehouse district. The street was full of luxury cars parked in tight spaces, juxtaposing the crumbling facades of the neighboring buildings.

A cool breeze calmly blew through the streets as the sound of techno music palpitated in the air. The bass rattled the organs in my body and took over the beating of my heart as I walked closer to the entrance. There was a small line and a bouncer guarding red velvet ropes.

"I'm here to meet Jacques," I said to the giant with a clipboard and ear piece. His black suit and purple silk dress shirt rippled with the Santa Ana winds.

"Haven't seen Jacques," he replied.

"He said you'd let me in if I mentioned his name," I said. "I'm supposed to meet him here."

"Yeah, well, Jacques' not here. You know his friend Benjamin?" He patted his pants pocket like a pushy bellhop.

I stood there awkwardly until I realized he wanted me to pay him to get in. I reached for my wallet and handed him a twenty. He motioned to the doorway.

"Tell Jacques I said 'Hello,'" he said. "And to bring me more of that booze."

The inside of the warehouse was dark, the air so thick with smoke I could only see about ten feet in front of me. Loud techno music thumped deeply in the ether of the slowly hovering smoke as strobe lights flashed to their own rhythm. The crowd, when I could see it at all, was young, elegant, fashionable, and quite obviously rich.

As I made my way to the bar on the other end of the room, I saw the two collectors from lunch taking shots. One of them looked over at me and whispered to the other. They both looked in my direction and laughed before hurrying off to avoid me. I guessed I wouldn't be selling them any paintings on this trip.

I ordered a martini and wandered around trying to find Dmitry or Jacques. I felt uncomfortable in this crowd. It was obvious I was alone, and every group of partiers I approached seemed to look at me with disdain, like I was some sort of undesirable cretin. I wondered if they could smell my middle class roots sprouting from my unshaven face. Or, more than likely, I looked like a narc with my mustache and trench coat to these hip, sophisticated elites. I wished I had more of Jacques's magical booze from earlier to ease my nerves in this inhospitable warehouse. I figured I'd order another drink and try my best to enjoy the weird vibes of the rave.

As I wandered back to the bar, I caught sight of Jacques, the strobe lights illuminating him briefly as he stood at the edge of the dance floor. I could swear he was staring at me, his mouth twisted into a smirk as our eyes met through the crowd. I tried to make my way towards him but the amorphous dance floor was so crowded that I kept running into disgruntled partiers while the fog machines kept pumping misty air. By the time I reached where Jacques had been standing, he was gone. He seemed to have disappeared into the crowd like a ghost.

Back at the bar, I sipped another martini and watched the attractive multitudes dancing all around me. One woman in particular caught my eye as she approached the bar to order a drink. I tried my best to muster a confident smile in her direction—but it came out more like a pathetic sneer. She stood next to me and her shoulder grazed my arm as her jet black hair glittered in the dark of the rave, reflecting the strobe lights that punctured the darkness along with the music's thumping bass. I got a good look at her. She wore a red cardigan over a white wife beater, a black bra, tight black jeans, and red heels. A black Chanel quilted backpack hung from her shoulders.

"A martini?" she said with a Russian accent, although I could barely hear her above all the ruckus.

"Oh, uh, yeah. What'd you order?" I said dashingly.

Her soft hand grazed mine, and said, "Same." She grinned devilishly. Her sienna eyes bore a hole into my heart as she looked me up and down, sizing me up. She then brought her hand to my waist, softly caressed my lower back as I felt a fever in my loins.

I nodded my head toward her, as a bashful grin overcame my face, not really certain why this was happening. Had she mistaken me for someone else? I was shocked this beautiful woman was talking to me, and that she seemed to be flirting with me. I wasn't used to this sort of attention from a stranger.

"What's your name?" I asked.

"Lada," she said, although I wasn't sure if I heard her correctly.

"Johnny," I said, as I gestured my hand to my heart to pledge allegiance to myself. I asked her if she knew Dmitry. She shook her head yes and began talking as the deafening sounds of the rave hammered above us. I just kept grinning, completely unable to hear what she said, staring at her face as my head continued bobbing up and down, pretending to make sense of her words. Finally, she grabbed my arm with a grin, and dragged me out of the rave. We passed the bouncer, who winked and saluted me. I couldn't believe this was happening.

We got to her car, a vintage gold Mercedes convertible from what I guessed was the late seventies. I worried about my rental car, which was still parked on a nearby street, but I didn't want to get in the way of whatever was happening. I kept quiet, and she sped off into the night, driving down Sunset, before turning onto Echo Park Avenue. She snaked up the hilly streets, weaving the car through the neighborhood. She pulled into a driveway at the top of a hill. I got out of the car, looked at the street corner, and saw what I thought might be a giant paved cliff, too steep to be a road.

"Is that an actual street?" I asked as I tried to imagine a car driving up it in the darkness.

She smiled, "That's Baxter Street. People drive up it all the time."

We walked up to a small bungalow with a weathered exterior while wind swept the scent of jasmine into my nose. I could hear coyotes howling in the nearby hills.

The inside of the house had been recently renovated, its worn facade disguising a modern interior. Immediately, I noticed the expensive art collection hanging on the walls: works by Mike Kelley, Paul McCarthy, John Baldessari, Laura Owens, John McCracken, Larry Bell, Vija Celmins, Ed Ruscha, and, of course, Dmitry Vaga. But before I could mention the impressive collection, she grabbed me by the shoulders and kissed me passionately. She then playfully pushed me away.

"Let me make you a drink," she said as she sauntered over to a liquor cart, grabbing a few bottles and walking to the kitchen.

I studied the works on the walls as I heard the sound of ice cubes dropping into two glasses. The Mike Kelley painting was stunning, depicting a green faced devil with golden horns and a bright red, forked tongue dangling from a menacing grimace. She mixed the drinks quickly and brought me the cocktail.

"It was so nice to meet you tonight, Johnny," she said. "Cheers."

"Cheers," I said as we clinked the glasses. I took a large gulp.

I gagged as the drink slid down my throat, and tasted an even stronger elixir than what I drank with Jacques earlier. After a few seconds, I felt my center of gravity abandoning me. As I stumbled, I caught myself by grabbing the wall next to the Mike Kelley painting to keep from falling over. My vision became cloudy as I slowly slid down the wall, dragging my shoulder and side of my face against it, dropping my drink, and finally landing on my side on the floor. I looked up at Lada, but she was mostly a blur. For a split moment my vision returned. I saw Lada's crossed arms as she studied me with detachment.

"What kind of drink was that?" I whispered, as a black puddle seeped from my peripheral vision towards my pupils and I drifted into the dark void.

I awoke with a devastating headache on the living room couch completely naked to the sounds of coffee being made in the kitchen. Despite my groggy head pounding, I felt a glistening relaxation throughout my body like I'd been given a heavy dose of opiates. My clothes were neatly folded on a chair next to me. What happened to me? How did I end up here? I remembered the drive to the house, but everything else was a dense fog. Did I get laid last night? I rubbed my crotch with my fingers and brought them up to sniff. It didn't smell like musky sex down there. I just smelled the sweat of alcohol and like I desperately needed a shower. What the fuck went on last night? I quickly dressed and followed the smell of coffee into the kitchen.

"Morning," Lada said.

"Uh, Morning," I said, pausing for a second to gather my thoughts. "So, I don't remember what happened last night, and I'm pretty embarrassed."

"You've got nothing to worry about," she said."You were a perfect gentleman, and I should have warned you I was making a strong drink. You just passed out. Luckily I was able to call my neighbor to help get you on the couch."

"I'm so sorry. I didn't realize I got that drunk last night. Is this your art collection?" I asked to change the subject.

"No," she said. "This isn't my house. The organization I work for owns it. I just stay here when I'm in town on business."

"It's a great collection," I said. "Who do you work for?"

"That's none of your business," she said.

"Oh, I'm sorry," I said. "I didn't mean to be rude. I was just curious. I'm an artist so I always like seeing a house full of art."

"You're an artist?" she said. "I don't like art."

I didn't say anything to that. I also didn't like most of the art I saw, but the house was full of art I actually did like.

She brought the coffee to the backyard where we sat on a marble bench facing west, staring into the hazy morning sky, sipping the delicious light roast, and smoking cigarettes. I could see a tiny sliver of the Pacific Ocean gleaming in the distance through a copse of Box Elder trees. I could've gotten used to spending my mornings this way despite my hangover, although I could tell Lada was annoyed by my presence. I couldn't blame her for that. Besides, I had a flight back to New York to catch.

She called me a cab so I could get back to my rental car and then head to the hotel to grab my things before my flight. She was elated to be rid of me, as though I was a chore that had been completed. I was confused by what had just occurred; I wasn't used to picking up attractive strangers at warehouse raves, and then passing out like a drunken asshole on the floor. I was sure we hadn't had sex, but I wondered if Lada was some sort of succubus, sent by a demonic, cosmic entity to suck the life force out of me. Or, maybe I was just a fucking idiot with a drinking problem.

4

Back in New York and cooped up in my studio painting, I'd
spent a lot of time thinking about my experience at Lada's
house. I'd never gotten so drunk that I'd fallen to the floor and
immediately passed out, especially when there was a chance
of getting laid. I began to wonder whether I'd been drugged. I
remembered her saying a neighbor helped get me to the couch.
But why had I woken up completely naked? I tried to ignore
these nagging thoughts as I painted, but the more I thought
about it, the more paranoid I felt. Whenever I left my loft, I
felt anxious and suspicious of every person I walked past on
the street.

Nonetheless, I had to get out of my studio after isolating myself for a few days making work. I found myself thirsty for some
booze and company, so I filled a flask with Scotch, smoked
a joint, and hit the streets of the Lower East Side. I walked
along the Bowery to East Houston, taking in the hundreds of
nameless humans walking past and listening to the many sam-

ples of voices and conversations streaming around me on the street. As I listened to the sounds of the city, I heard something else: the sound of footsteps behind me. There was something about the sound that made me stop in my tracks, as though I could sense danger hovering in the air just above the surface of everything in sight. A feeling of intense disquiet overcame me. I'd been back in town for less than a week, but the city had already erased the relaxed vibes I'd acquired during my trip to Los Angeles.

I turned around at Ludlow and locked eyes with a man in a dark trench coat and baseball cap who appeared to be taking too much of an interest in me. I wondered if he had been tailing me. I ducked into a doorway and lit a cigarette, waiting for the man to pass by. As he walked by, I caught his glance once again as he turned to walk into a dusty bodega. Paranoia enveloped my thoughts. But why the fuck would anybody be following me? I couldn't shake the creepy feeling though. I waited, hoping I'd see him emerge from the bodega to continue on his way, but after ten minutes of waiting and nervously smoking, I abandoned the fruitless endeavor, and my anxiety along with it. I realized how badly I needed to get out of my studio and socialize. Maybe it hadn't been the best idea to smoke a joint before I went out.

I said "Hey" to the doorman Carlo, showed him my ID, shook his hand, and walked into Max Fish. Inside, the smoky bar's pink lighting cast a cloudy glow over the dark narrow room as pinball machines dinged and the Replacements blared from the jukebox. There was a strange hushed tone to the bar patrons's conversations that didn't seem to match the normal sort of debauchery I was accustomed to at Max Fish. It was as though the room was trying to recover from a cataclysmic event. As I eavesdropped at the bar, I thought I could hear Martin's name on the tips of every patron's tongue. I spotted my least favorite artist acquaintance, a skater and graffiti dude like most of the regulars at Max Fish. Whenever I saw his face, I couldn't help but picture his boring, fake Basquiat paintings hanging in my mind. As he approached, I geared up for another meaningless conversation.

"You hear about that German artist dude Martin?" he asked, as the cotton candy neon lighting illuminated his face by the bar.

"Kippenberger?" I asked.

"Yeah. He just swung from a chandelier, flew off, and crashed into a table. He almost broke some woman's ankle, fucking idiot. He got thrown out. I heard he's a dick."

He saw another one of his friends who also made terrible graffiti-influenced paintings, nodded to him, and stumbled away. I imagined they had a bag of coke, and were headed to the bathroom for some more bumps to speed up the erasure of the night.

Knowing Martin might be near, I left the bar to search for him, wandering the Lower East Side like a search-and-rescue dog sniffing for his scent. Within ten minutes, my ears perked up at the sound of shouting. Further down Rivington, I saw a man drunkenly dancing and screaming like he'd just escaped from the loony bin. As I approached, Martin began swinging around a light post as elegantly as Fred Astaire.

"Johnny, you fuck!" he yelled when he saw me.

"What are you doing back in the city?" I asked.

"A show, and some business!" he said.

He swayed, inebriated, as he pulled a flask from his trench coat. He took a giant gulp, and passed me the booze. I gladly accepted. The white lightning thundered down my throat, and my body felt weightless immediately, a sense of euphoria flooding my mind. Whenever I drank from Martin's flask, I noticed my vision began to do some weird shit. It looked as though one of Martin's eyes was bobbing back and forth like a buoy in the ocean, and his face had morphed into a ghastly yellow mask in which his eyes burned red.

"I've been meaning to ask—what the fuck are we drinking? Absinthe or something?"

"It's an IPA. A very strong beer!" Martin said.

"IPA? What the fuck is that? It tastes stronger than absinthe." I put my hand on his shoulder to keep from falling over. I guessed the IPA, whatever the fuck it was, was working.

"You know Jacques?" he asked.

"Yeah, I think I met him in L.A.," I answered, not particularly happy to be reminded of meeting Gesualdo's double.

Martin's eyes focused on me. "Well, we need to see him. He owes me money. And if he can't pay, then he can at least quench our thirst. He's got a lot of this IPA stored at my studio. He should be there now." He put his arm around my shoulder and pulled me with him into the uncertain night. I wasn't excited to see Jacques again, but I did want to get a look at Martin's studio.

We walked along Delancey for a while and then turned on Allen, zig-zagging through the streets. Usually, I had a good sense of direction, but following Martin around made my internal compass whirl in confusion. Throughout our journey, Martin continued to pass me his flask. I watched the nighttime bacchants all around us drink and party their way through the streets, the sound of car horns providing a soundtrack to their frenzied activities. It seemed as though even the buildings had begun to smile as I drank more from Martin's flask and saw faces in the bricks around us. The buildings grinned down at us like friendly carnival masks, as though they were glad we were enjoying ourselves in their company.

Finally, we arrived in an alleyway in Chinatown. Steam rose from the sewers as though they were breathing. At first,

I smelled piss and shit wafting up with the mist, but then an impossibly sugary, pastry smell penetrated my sinuses. Martin stopped at a doorway.

"Ready for a studio visit?" he asked as he opened the door.

"Yes!" flew out of my mouth, and we walked up a rickety metal staircase, stopping four flights up. Maybe it was just Kippenberger's beer, but it seemed like the door in front of us had appeared out of nowhere. Martin turned the knob and gingerly opened the door.

We walked into a huge loft, grand but crumbling. There were pallets of boxes everywhere, arranged like a maze. One corner seemed to be an art studio, but there were no works in progress. The paintings lining the corner of the room were wrapped in opaque plastic so I could only make out the color schemes and outlines of the paintings inside. Wooden crates full of sculptures were arranged neatly. Nearby was a scraggly bed with sheets messed about. I was so absorbed in trying to look at the work that I didn't realize Martin had disappeared.

As I wandered through the maze of boxes, I followed the sound of voices to the corner of the loft where I found Martin talking to a woman I'd never seen before. She elegantly smoked a cigarette and looked like Marlene Dietrich with her curly blonde hair that hung just above her shoulders, blue eyes sitting below perfectly plucked eyebrows, and lips painted maroon. I watched as she took a drink straight from a bottle of whiskey. They were speaking in German. I couldn't tell whether the conversation was hostile or friendly. The guttural German barking was hard to make any sense of, and reminded me of feeling like an uncultured idiot in Cologne.

Even though I couldn't understand a word that was being said, I could tell the woman carried herself with authority and spoke with a sharp-witted sultriness. I wondered if she was Martin's girlfriend. Maybe it was the IPA flooding his cheeks, but Martin appeared to be blushing. I was blushing too as I stared at the woman's profile, already a bit in love with that side of her. When she noticed me staring, she stopped speaking and turned to get a better look at me. Meanwhile, Martin stood in the corner, hands behind his back, staring thoughtfully out the window into the alley below, looking like one of his most famous sculptures.

Martin turned around, and said, "Johnny, this is my associate. We need help getting these boxes out of here."

"I'm Johnny Dabs," I said to the woman, hoping to have the opportunity to put a name to her enchanting face. She just stared at me and said nothing. I looked at Martin dumbly, feeling slightly embarrassed by the snub.

"Would you be willing to let us store some of these pallets at your studio for a fee?" Martin asked.

I was confused, but my instinct was to help in any way I could.

"We'll pay you for your help," Martin continued. "How about $20,000 to store them for about a month?"

Dollar signs exploded from my eyeballs. "Sure," I said. I needed the money. I still hadn't been fully paid for all the work I'd sold in Cologne. After all, my bank account needed to be replenished after all my jet setting.

"Jacques will arrange a time to drop them off within the week," Martin said. "We appreciate your help."

"What's in the boxes?" I asked. I was glad to help, but also curious.

"It's beer. IPA, like we drank earlier." Martin said, and passed me the flask.

"When do I get paid?" I asked, taking a sip from the flask and immediately feeling myself go cross-eyed.

"She'll write you a check right now," Martin said. "I have to leave. I've got business to tend to. Thanks for seeing the studio."

Martin made his exit, leaving me alone with the mysterious German woman. Her thick blonde hair flipped as she turned to look at me. She didn't look impressed.

"I didn't catch your name," I said to her.

"No names," she said, as she stood in front of me with a checkbook and pen. "Only your name. How's it spelled?" I felt the alcohol on her breath rush out of her mouth like opening a furnace door.

"You said 'no names,'" I said in an attempt to flirt.

"Do you want this check, or no?" she asked, still unimpressed.

"Johnny Dabs. It's spelled J, O, H, N, N, Y. The last name is D, A, B, S," I replied.

She tore out the check, and as she handed it to me, I noticed her fingernails were painted black. I had no inkling what was in store for me. I just liked money. Where was the harm in that?

It was six-thirty in the morning when I left, so I walked around the city for a while to stay awake and then rushed to the bank at eight and noticed—while waiting in line—my name printed on the check from a computer. I'd thought the German woman was writing my name on the check when she asked me to spell it. The top left hand corner of the check read "Congress for Russian Cultural Freedom LLC." I wondered what the fuck kind of business was paying me, but figured I shouldn't dwell on anything other than getting the money into my bank account. I deposited the check and the teller congratulated me on my fortune with a toothy grin. I took out some cash, and later that night bought myself a bottle of expensive Scotch to celebrate. As I walked out of the liquor store triumphantly, I realized I hadn't seen Jacques at Martin's studio. Where was Jacques, and why the fuck was I somehow involved with that sleazy Gesualdo-looking motherfucker?

5

Two weeks after depositing the check, I arrived at my studio after getting some drinks at Max Fish, and found myself unable to open the door. Confused, I pushed with all my might, but the door wouldn't budge any further than a foot or so. I stuck my head in, and almost headbutted a wall of boxes that I recognized as the booze from Martin's studio. While I'd been out, the maze of IPA had taken over my loft. I shimmied my way into the room through the cracked door and found the boxes had been stacked so tall that I couldn't see over them. I hugged the wall, inching slowly, as I looked for a way to penetrate the space.

As I got to the first corner of the loft from the door, I saw the row of boxes ended a few feet from my bed. I continued to creep along the wall until I got to my bed, and tried to orient myself to this new reality. I stood on my bed to get a better view. Once I got my bearings, I counted ten rows of twenty pallets, perfectly arranged into a rectangle taking up all the free space

in the front half of my loft. The furniture had been relocated
and stacked in a corner to accommodate the pallets of booze.
Luckily, the corner of my studio where I worked and the corner
opposite where I slept, were mostly untouched.

As I approached my bed, I noticed a Kippenberger painting
wrapped in the same opaque plastic as the work in his studio
leaning against the foot of my bed. A note was taped to the face
of the wrapped painting. It read:

J. DABS!

ENJOY THE PAINTING FOR YOUR TROUBLES. ALSO
BOOKS POSTERS BOOZE FOR YOU.

A REAL FELLOW SEEKS AND STRIVES AND DOES
NOT COMPLAIN ABOUT IT BUT IS HAPPY IN THE
UNHAPPINESS OF THE RISING BUT NEVER ARRIVING
LINE OF LIFE. THAT IS THE HIGHEST FLOOR WE
CAN REACH. BUT EVERYTHING ELSE, THE DOG
SHIT ON THE GROUND FLOOR OF LIFE—THAT'S
WHAT WE'RE TALKING ABOUT . . . WE ARE BORN
TO SEEK, TO UNRAVEL KNOTS, TO SEE THE WORLD
FROM A WORM'S EYE POINT OF VIEW.

GO AHEAD AND KEEP PAINTING, JUST DON'T
HURT YOURSELF.

HA!

KIPPI

I scrambled to find a blade to unwrap the painting. When I removed the plastic, I saw it was a diptych in a frame. A self-portrait painted in red and white, in which Martin's hands were
bound in a plastic beer ring. A single unopened beer dangled
between his constricted hands. In the painting, Martin looked
captive to the booze, his hands raised in surrender as though
he were gearing up for torture, his face appearing both fearful

and aware of what was to come.

When I finally looked away from the painting, I noticed a stack of books and exhibition posters from Martin's many shows had been placed on the other side of my bed. And, of course, on top of the pile there was a bottle of the infamous IPA I'd become accustomed to drinking with Martin. There was no label, but IPA was silkscreened in white on the green bottle.

As I grabbed the bottle from its place on the bed for a celebratory drink, I heard the sound of something scurrying, and then a crash from the nucleus of the pallets. I put the bottle down and turned to look at the wall of boxes. I assumed it was a rat. I was currently the only tenant that occupied the building, other than the rats that frequented my dwelling. I liked to think of them as friends over for a studio visit rather than something to despair over.

I popped open the bottle and took a giant gulp of the harsh liquor. A calm washed over me as the IPA flowed down my throat.

After about thirty minutes of drinking and studying my recent acquisitions, I noticed a shadow had appeared on the wall. I watched as it morphed into a breathing being, one that looked like some sort of demon detective, complete with a fedora and a trench coat that resembled my own favorite coat. The ghost hovered and stared down at me as he floated a foot above the boxes of booze. His translucent skin appeared to be shifting between shades of blue randomly. I shook my head but the ghost still hovered patiently. The more I looked at him, the more familiar his face seemed. His face was young and his eyes were icy blue, but his body looked like that of a forty-five year old man. He was looking at me, but his gaze seemed to focus beyond me. Then I realized who he looked like.

"Are you Rimbaud?" I asked the demon.

He said nothing, just continued to float.

"You're Arthur Rimbaud," I said. "I just want you to know how much your work means to me. I love you." I was obsessed with Arthur Rimbaud. I'd long been fascinated by a portrait of him taken when he was sixteen years old with a faraway gaze and a disgruntled but angelic face. He was my favorite poet and his book *Illuminations* was like my version of the Bible.

He continued his silence, but I wanted him to speak to me. I knew he wasn't just some vision. He was too real to be a figment of my imagination. I felt the need to touch him to make sure I wasn't imagining him.

"You're Rimbaud," I said. "I know you're Rimbaud."

The demon shook his head. I was glad he had finally acknowledged me.

"Don't be scared," I said. "I'm gonna climb up there with you. I just want to shake your hand. No funny business, I promise."

I grabbed a ladder from the corner of my studio and brought it to the edge of the boxes as the demon detective continued to silently watch me from above. I began to climb up the ladder and cautiously placed my foot on one of the boxes to test its sturdiness. It felt stable, so I began to step off of the ladder, putting my weight onto the center of the box. I looked back at the demon and as he shook his head again, I felt my foot slip, the ladder falling to its side, as I tumbled off the box onto the floor. I landed on my side and felt the hard concrete. It didn't hurt that bad. I guessed the IPA was a nice pain reliever.

I lay there for a few seconds in a daze before attempting to get back up. The demon still hovered calmly above me.

"I'm a fucking idiot," I said to the demon. "Sorry about that." Before I could say anything more, he had vanished.

"Jesus fucking Christ," I said to myself.

I went to my bed to lay down, but it felt like I was sinking into the bed. Immediately, I thought of Martin and all of our interactions, and a strange electricity flowed through my body.

I was exhausted, but also energized. As I stared up at my ceiling, a persian rug appeared, breathing along with my breath. It undulated, ebbing and flowing like waves on the shore. Then, a black glam rocker boot looking like a David Bowie B-side began stomping on the rug.

The hallucinations didn't bother me. I felt calm, in awe of the visions. There was a feeling deep inside me telling me to trust my eyes. The visions disappeared after half an hour, and I was left alone with sleepiness. I leaned over on the side of the bed, kissed the portrait of Gesualdo, and tried to fall asleep.

I saw the demon detective from the shadow world flying away from me, orchestrating a war like a symphony conductor. I heard music flowing through his hands as they moved to and fro, controlling the sounds emanating from his being. I was then on the ground in a dark trench, as explosions erupted around me. Then, the demon was in the trench motioning for me to follow him. As I moved toward him, he started to run. I chased him down spiraling steps. When I got to the bottom, he was in a dungeon, locked up behind bars. He was looking down with his fedora hiding his face. As I got closer, he looked into my eyes. I recognized my own face looking back at me. The demon detective took off his trench coat and revealed a gun in his hand. He pointed it at me and shot. A giant wave engulfed me, and I was washed up on the shore like a beached whale. A seagull circled above me squawking, and then dive bombed right toward my head. I threw my hands up in terror, and screamed.

I awoke. It was noon.

6

I know my story, as I've recounted it thus far, is full of jet-setting success—flying across the ocean to Germany, taking a trip to L.A. just to see if I could sell some paintings—but, my life in New York didn't start out that way, and hadn't been that way for very long. In fact, these were the first moments of success in a career full of desperate attempts to get my foot in the door.

When I first moved to New York in 1989 to "make it" as an artist, I was very naive as to how much the universe didn't give a shit about my romantic ideals surrounding art and life. I was twenty-two years old, and believed that the work I made mattered in some lofty, cosmic sense. My paintings, drawings, and zines were all that mattered to me. I didn't think my work was going to change the world. But I believed if a gallery would just take a chance on me and represent my work, then I could truly make great things. I lived in a civilization of images and that's where I wanted to make my mark.

Before moving to New York, I had been living in Houston,

Texas where I studied art at a local university. After I graduated, I began getting involved with the local art scene, going to every opening, befriending the artists whose work I admired, meeting collectors, and doing my best to get to know the curators of all the local museums. Around that time, I had a solo show of my paintings at a friend's house gallery, and sold the show out. A few months later, I won a very large cash prize for a drawing I'd made. Feeling like I had conquered the provincial scene, I decided to try my luck in New York City.

Needless to say, things weren't so easy in New York. It felt like the hustle and bustle of New York's vast art scene bitch-slapped me back to reality within a few months of arriving there. The money I'd saved vanished before my eyes, and before long, I had to find work. The jobs I worked barely covered my meager living expenses. The first two years were very difficult, and I almost moved back to Houston with my tail between my legs like a cowed mutt numerous times. But mustering all of my strength, I made it work. I slowly made friends and networked with other artists as we mounted our own art shows in abandoned storefronts in the Lower East Side and Brooklyn.

During this time, the New York art world was retracting after the bubble of frenzied speculation in the 80s had burst. The galleries in the East Village and SoHo were the nexus of the scene but it wasn't the 80s anymore, and by the mid-90s, many galleries were shuttering their doors and going out of business. Since I had arrived at the tail end of this era, it was nearly impossible to find a dealer who was willing to take a chance on an unknown artist like me. But I knew each artist had to create their own path. There was no right way to go about being a successful artist, no manual to consult to resuscitate a flailing art career. I tried to get in on the scene by drinking at the right bars, meeting the right people, and wooing the right dealers and collectors. But it was incredibly difficult to navigate this mysterious little world.

Back then, I'd often go gallery hopping in SoHo to check out the shows and see the works chosen by the art gods themselves. After a few shows, I'd get hungry, and if I felt like I had a little cash to throw around, I'd splurge on a sandwich at Dean & DeLuca. I'd sit at the window, watching the street where I'd inevitably see some poor sad-sack artist walk by with a box of slides under his arm, psyching himself up to present his work to the uninterested gallerinas and gallerinos. It became like watching a sport. Sometimes, I'd even follow the aspiring artist into an intimidating gallery and watch as he stammered an introduction to the indifferent gatekeepers of their dreams. It never went well, and the downtrodden artist would walk out with shameful defeat in their eyes.

Meanwhile, the artists finding success were young, hip, and equipped with Master's degrees from Yale, CalArts, RISD, Columbia, Hunter, or any other place where you could pay six figures to get connections. They made reactionary work against the bubble of speculation around Neo-Expressionist paintings from the preceding decade. Installation art and conceptual painting were all the rage. I'd go to an opening at an up and coming gallery only to find pieces of paper pinned to the wall sloppily, graphite drawings etched directly on the walls. Or, some paintings depicting lazy, provisional abstraction—a brush stroke here, a line of spray paint in the upper corner. Nothing looked completed, or like it took much effort. And then there was a price list at the front desk with some heady, complicated, philosophical explanation to justify why the work looked like shit. Or, even worse, there'd be some obtuse, awkward performance on opening night. All the shows ran together, and I simply didn't get it. I was a painter and drawer, and I didn't care if people thought what I was doing was boring or retrograde.

But the thing that these "revolutionary" hipster artists didn't understand was that art had always been an excuse for rich people to decorate their homes. Did these artists think wealthy collectors wanted to buy a bunch of trash that looked like it was gathered from the gutters of Alphabet City to put above their $30,000 couch? Although this fact clashed with some of my ideals, I didn't mind delivering one of my paintings to some hedge fund Gordon Gecko asshole as long as the money was right. Being alive is expensive, and living in New York certainly wasn't cheap.

During my first five years in New York, I was very poor and very unhappy. Then, about two years before this story begins, I started selling work on a regular basis. I had no dealer, but all of a sudden, I was selling paintings, the wheels of fortune spinning wildly toward a jackpot. I was finally in a position to quit my shitty jobs in order to focus on making work. I felt lucky, but I figured my luck was a byproduct of my hard work. I felt proud to be in the position I was in.

This was around the time I decided I needed a better studio than my bedroom. My hope was to find a loft big enough to function as both a studio and a home. I started asking around, putting it into the air that I was looking for a space. Then one day, a collector of mine said he might know of an available property. He gave me the phone number of one of his colleagues at JP Morgan, who he said owned a lot of real estate and had a soft spot for creatives. He offered me a bargain that was beyond comprehension: In lieu of asking me to pay a monthly rent to live in the loft, he asked only for a painting for each month I lived there. Twelve paintings per year. I eagerly agreed to the deal. I thought I might've been the luckiest man in New York at that moment.

The property was on Great Jones, a weird little street I had often found myself drawn to during the first couple of years of my life in New York. Back then, in order to get out of my numerous shitty apartments and away from the shitty roommates I lived with, I'd wander aimlessly around the city. I fancied myself a Situationist and was obsessed with Guy Debord's book *The Society of the Spectacle*, as well as the many booklets, novels, films, artworks and communiques the group created in the late sixties and early seventies. I'm still not quite certain what it actually meant to be a Situationist in the year 1996, but I often wandered the streets on a dérive, allowing chance to lead my way. On these walks, I kept ending up on Great Jones Street, historically a hotbed for junkies in New York's seedy, bohemian past. Andy Warhol even owned the building that Basquiat overdosed in, which was a few doors down from my loft. The small street was still transitioning from a drug haven to being a fraction less frightening. I didn't mind all that, as long as nobody fucked with me.

The loft on Great Jones was a dream come true for me. Sure, there were junkies and derelicts roaming my street at all times, but the loft was exactly what I needed. I knew this was going to be the place where my art career finally took off. I just didn't know it'd one day be filled with stacks of boxes containing IPA.

7

A month after the IPA took over my studio, I put on a Lightnin'
Hopkins record, and sat drinking some on my couch, while I
smoked a joint and reflected on all the unusual things I'd been
seeing lately.

Ever since the IPA had come into my life, normal booze simply didn't take me to where I wanted to go anymore. When I
drank the strange brew, objects seemed to vibrate as I looked
at them, and the most banal things swept me away with won-
derment. Like the other day when I stood on Mott staring at a
Callery Pear tree, completely mesmerized by the life breathing
out of it as it swayed and danced with Being. A tree had never
seemed more full of life, and I wondered what the tree's name
was. There wasn't a question in my mind that it wouldn't have
a name. It was too ebullient to be just another tree, and, in
that moment, I realized I was surrounded by exuberant trees
everywhere in New York. I had just never taken the time to
notice them. From then on, I said "hello" to all of the trees

on my walk home. I shook their hands, feeling their leaves in my paws.

It was as though the IPA offered me an awareness and appreciation for the things I usually took for granted. When I was drinking, the things I saw were scrubbed of their familiarity, and made brand new. I felt like a child in awe of the world and its tiny wonders. I realized things, like trees, bushes, and the flowerbeds that surrounded them, were universes unto themselves, living beings concerned with their own existences and survival. But the IPA also made me see a sinister reality beneath them I'd never noticed before. It was like I had discovered some secret code that was obviously there, but I couldn't decipher. And that frightened me a little bit, but then some new thing would sweep me away and I'd forget my creeping paranoia. Beyond the strange visions, I felt a luminous relaxation and elation in my body. I felt like I was made of clouds. I never felt sloppy drunk—although I knew I was drunk as shit—just very subdued and relaxed, despite the intensity of the things I saw. Everything felt overflowing with festivity despite some of the ominous feelings I felt lurking deep within me. I wondered if the visions were conjured by the stresses of my existence. Even with my rent covered, the costs of living and making work in New York were brutal, and I was always scrambling for money to make my next batch of paintings.

I got up and flipped the record to listen to the other side of the Lightnin' Hopkins LP, sat my cloud body back on the cloud couch, and floated off with Lightnin' as my guide. When the record finished, I poured some IPA into my flask, and stepped out onto Great Jones, lit a cigarette, took a gulp of IPA, and investigated the street. Calm. Normal.

I planned to have a leisurely stroll and eventually head to Last Bacall, my favorite bar in the whole world, to meet my artist friends for a drink, to talk shit and catch up. For the last couple of weeks, I'd noticed wheat-pasted advertisements for a blockbuster Dmitry Vaga show at Gagosian Gallery in SoHo, which was scheduled to open the next evening. The posters were everywhere in the city. Everyone was talking about the show, and it was an unavoidable topic of conversation amongst all the artist losers like me. None of my friends liked his work. In fact, a ton of energy was spent talking about what a shitty artist he was, especially among my comrades, all of whom were toiling in obscurity, desperate for even a sliver of the notoriety Dmitry enjoyed.

The poster for the show was a shadowy silhouette of Dmitry in profile, dressed in his trademark black turtleneck, Wayfarers, his curly hair messed about, and a smokey, gray background behind him decorated with a grid of Chanel logos. In white block letters in the center of the poster: DMITRY VAGA. Below that in red letters: GAGOSIAN GALLERY. Below that in yellow letters at the bottom: THE CHANEL FLOWER PAINTINGS. The poster was part Warhol, part Russian propaganda poster, part Bob Dylan in 1965. I thought to myself: fuck Dmitry Vaga.

Dmitry had some endorsement deal with Chanel. This fact made us all roll our eyes in disgust, and a faint rumbling of sour vomit burned in my guts every time I saw the stupid fucking posters around the city. Meanwhile, there was fawning press for Dmitry in all the major art publications. Even critics who'd usually rail against this sort of endorsement deal with a luxury brand seemed excited to see what the young art star had to show. The posters on Great Jones were too much for me to handle. I doubted the sales team at Gagosian would want any of the dead-eyed miscreants from my block to attend.

As I reached the Bowery, I noticed two incredibly handsome men that looked out of place. They backed into a doorway as they saw me approaching. I remembered it was the same spot Martin had been abducted after our first meeting. They weren't the men who had put Martin in the back of the car, but I'd seen them around the neighborhood in their perfectly tailored suits, their modelly faces with perfectly high cheekbones, and their perfectly styled hair. Something about them put me on red alert, but they seemed to ignore me as I passed by, headed toward Spring Street.

I wasn't sure why, but the men made me feel paranoid. I'd noticed them before, but couldn't understand why they were there. Only five other people seemed to live on the block besides me and the junkie squatters lounging around. They were way too handsome to be cops. I wondered if they were real estate agents looking to buy some of the buildings to gentrify the neighborhood. The more I thought about it, the more I realized I'd noticed them almost the whole time I'd lived on Great Jones. I lit another cigarette and decided to try to ignore my paranoia. Getting drunk with my friends was more important than unearthing the mystery of some handsome yuppies.

The dark wooden walls of Last Bacall were covered with images of Lauren Bacall—film stills, promotional headshots, paparazzi photos, Bogey and Bacall walking hand in hand, Bacall smoking a cigarette. The pictures alone were enough to make me a returning customer, since Bacall was one of my favorite Old Hollywood crushes, but the bar was also famed for its cheap and ineffably strong drinks. It was usually crawling with artists, writers, junkies, ne'er-do-wells, bohemians, and other undesirables. Inside, I saw my good bud D'Angelo drinking alone in a booth, smoke curling around him in the neon glow illuminating the other patrons already in the midst of drinking themselves silly. John Coltrane played softly above the bar's chatter.

At the bar, I ordered a gin martini before heading to D'Angelo's booth to get the shit-talking party started.

"Fuck Dmitry Vaga," D'Angelo said as I sat down across from him in the booth.

"Jesus, man, those fucking posters are everywhere," I said.

"You went to his compound in L.A. right?"

"Yeah, I went to this weird rave that Dmitry hosted," I said. "I didn't see him there, but it was a weird scene. The compound was fucking huge. I wish I had that much space."

"That's L.A., man. Wide open spaces, sunshine, Hollywood."

"I met this weird Russian dude out there named Jacques," I said. "He sort of invited me to the party, but he wasn't there when I went. I think I saw him for a split second, but he disappeared into thin air. I don't know what his deal is, but I guess he's involved with the art world. He knows Kippenberger. I got bad vibes. He looks like Gesualdo's doppelgänger, too."

"Gesualdo's that weird composer you're always talking about?" D'Angelo asked. "That's some creepy music."

"Yeah, that's him. I gotta take a piss, I'll be right back," I said as I raced off.

When I got back from the bathroom, my friend Elena was sitting across from D'Angelo. These two were my favorite little crew in the world. We'd become inseparable, often going to openings, bars, and afterparties as a unit. They were both great painters, and great friends. Plus, Elena sort of resembled Monica Vitti. Her thick, wavy red hair cascaded like a waterfall down to her shoulders, straight bangs cut across her inviting face, giving support to an aquiline nose. She was Chilean, with green, sparkly eyes hiding the depth of her vast intellect. Beauty aside, I loved her work and had tremendous respect for her wit. Her career was beginning to skyrocket—she made haunting figurative paintings and portraits that looked like Symbolist nightmares from the underworld—and she fucking deserved it.

I wouldn't have admitted it then, but I had a major crush on her. We'd become close over the last two years. She had connections and would often go out of her way to help me out, like when she set up my visit to the Getty villa to see "Christ's Entry into Brussels." While I secretly pined for her, I had also met the stream of incredibly impressive men she dated—doctors, lawyers, finance guys, famous authors—all dreamy as could be and a million times more respectable than my loser ass. I knew I stood no chance to date her in any universe. Besides, I valued our friendship too much to risk an advance.

"Hey, Johnny," Elena said. "We were just saying, 'Fuck Dmitry Vaga' in a loop, over and over again."

"Seriously, fuck that little twerp," I said in solidarity, as I sat next to Elena in the booth. "The opening will be fun at least, good people watching." I tried to keep it on the sunny side as I lit up a cigarette.

Eduardo, another friend, joined us in our booth. He was a writer whose recent critically-acclaimed postmodern spy novel had been climbing up the *Times* bestseller list. He liked to hang out with artists, and was a constant presence around the scene. He moved freely between the literati and the art world, writing reviews for *ArtForum*, curating art shows at the trendiest galleries as a side gig, and stuffing his pockets in the process. He also enjoyed the bohemian gossip we were all so glad to spew.

"Johnny, I've been meaning to talk to you," Eduardo said.

"What's up?"

"I'm working on curating a show at Pat Hearn. I think you'd be perfect for it. I showed Pat your work. She loved it."

"Oh, that'd be sick," I said. "I'd love to show with her."

"I want to bring her by your studio in a few weeks."

"Anytime, man," I said, brimming with joy at the thought.

Eduardo and I set a time for a visit.

"I hear you and Kippenberger are inseparable now," Elena said.

"Not really," I said. "I met him at an opening in Alphabet City, hung out with him in Cologne. I keep running into him. It's been cool. I'm such a huge fan. It's weird, we've sort of become friends."

"I heard he gave you a painting," Eduardo said, eyeing me with interest. I was weirded out that Eduardo knew about it. I hadn't seen anyone since I got the painting and pallets of booze. I certainly hadn't told anyone about it. I supposed Martin had told some people. Maybe he was still in town. Maybe he'd be at Dmitry's opening the next night.

"Yeah, a self-portrait. I can't believe he gave it to me."

We continued to drink and gossip. Every once in a while, I'd sneak outside for some fresh air, but mainly because I was feeling too overheated in the bar. Outside the street was desolate. I took a few sips from the flask of IPA I'd been carrying in my pocket and watched a Pepsi can skitter by, blown by a cool breeze. Nearby, a trash can lay idly on its side, looking as though it was too drunk to stand. Everything around me gleamed as the streetlights overhead cast a yellow tint on the surfaces of everything in sight. The visions intensified as I took more pulls from my flask of IPA and lit a cigarette.

As I finished my cigarette, I noticed two men hovering in the shadows across the street. They looked like wealthy, young finance men that'd taken a wrong turn on their way home from Wall Street. I couldn't tell if they were the same guys from my block, but I still eyed them warily as I felt paranoid. They stopped their conversation as they took notice of me. Maybe they really were lost. I took another pull from the flask, and wondered if maybe I was the one that was lost. I was so shaken up by their presence and whether they were the same men I saw on my block earlier that I left the bar without even telling my friends goodbye, knowing I'd see them at Dmitry's opening the next night. As I walked up Mercer, I kept looking over my shoulder to make sure I wasn't being followed. Something sinister hung in the cold air. I couldn't place where it was coming from, but it was there.

8

Before Dmitry's opening, I tried to tidy up my studio a bit, but the pallets of booze made my attempts futile because there was no place to put anything. Defeated by the impossible task, I sat down on my bed and grabbed the bottle of IPA.

I felt incredibly anxious before big social events and had to prepare myself for being in a huge crowd of pretentious aesthetes. I hated all these art openings, but it was important to be present at shows like Dmitry's. You never knew who you might meet at an opening—some dealer, a big-time collector, some new friend or lover with a trust fund—the possibilities were limitless. You had to be there to find out. Maybe tonight I'd be able to introduce myself to Dmitry. I looked down at the bottle and thought of Martin. I had a feeling he might be at the show and I was excited to see him. I raised the bottle to my lips and drank deeply, bracing for the inevitable cough from the booze's overwhelming strength. Time slowed and a feeling of warmth cascaded through my body.

After a few more sips, I heard the sound of something moving from the depths of the pallets. I watched as the demon detective rose once again from the center of the maze of boxes. This time, though, his face no longer resembled Rimbaud's. It was like he'd aged thirty years since the last time I saw him. A five o'clock shadow covered his face. He now resembled Humphrey Bogart. He hovered above the boxes, glaring down at me, and then raised his arm into the air, pointing at the door.

"Are you a shape-shifting entity?" I asked.

He said nothing.

"What happened to Rimbaud?" I said. "You don't look like him anymore."

He said nothing but continued to stare at me as he floated near the ceiling.

"Are you Humphrey Bogart?" I asked. "Should I call you Bogey?"

And then he faded away. What the fuck was I seeing? What was happening to me?

Then I noticed the time. I would have to hurry if I wanted to make it to the opening. I changed real fast, grabbed my keys and trench coat, and ran out the door. A moment later, I ran back, found my trusty flask on my bed, poured the rotgut inside until it overflowed a bit, and licked the spilled booze off the body of the flask.

As I rushed toward the overhyped opening, I realized it felt like my eyes were levitating above the crowds in the street, as though I had a bird's eye view of everything before me. My body was definitely on the ground, but my eyes seemed to have jumped out of their sockets and reached far above my head as I drifted toward my destination. I floated down Broadway above the pedestrians and hubbub of the street. I watched as the sidewalk's bags of trash came alive, dancing with an electric current as I turned down Prince. The tops of heads bumbled and bounced, keeping time with the shuffling footsteps, looking like ants from my great height, all movements manufactured toward some utilitarian mission of collective order hidden beneath the surface of things. An old, dirty white van roared up Wooster, hitting every bump, sounding like a snare drum with every imperfection in the road, thundering an irregular beat. I felt light and airy.

As I approached the gallery, I noticed pedestrians gawking at me. I must have looked like a delirious psychopath as I inched toward the mass of people flocking to the opening on Wooster. I found myself back on the ground, walking with the mortals, no longer drifting above them. I guessed the booze was wearing off, but I still felt pretty wasted. Crowds were hanging listlessly outside, smoking cigarettes, making the scene, casting unwelcome grimaces to those not versed in the hermetic codes of those in the know.

In the gallery, I immediately walked over to the painting closest to the door, pretended to take it in without really looking at it, and then turned around to assess the scene. Hung on the gallery's glaringly white walls were ten huge paintings, all the same size, about eight feet tall, and ten feet wide. The images were uniform: Chanel logos silkscreened on top of realistically drafted flowers in vases, with spray painted lines indiscriminately obscuring portions of the canvas. God, they were lame as shit. And of course, the paintings' color schemes were all different, to match all sorts of million dollar couches.

I scanned the crowd for familiar faces, and saw a few movie stars; some young model waifs; a bunch of loser artists like myself; fancy finance bros; collector types; conservative-looking curators; art consultants; a bunch of old hipster heads; and plenty of young ones looking to take their rightful places in this snobbish milieu. It was definitely a star-studded affair, and after taking another quick look at the canvases on the wall, I finally noticed D'Angelo and Elena huddled in a corner. I tried to make my way over to them but the crowd was so thick that for every movement forward I made, I was pushed in the opposite direction twofold. After five minutes of impeded progress, I decided to let the crowd move me, drifting through the room like an abandoned boat in the sea. I reached for my flask in my trench coat pocket, took a sip, and coughed a bit as the crowd kept pushing me back.

My shoulder bumped into something behind me. I turned to apologize to whoever I'd run into, but instead of seeing a person, I saw a huge Dmitry Vaga painting falling toward me. My flask dropped from my hands and made a loud crash as it fell to the ground, IPA spilling all over the concrete floor. The canvas hit me in the head as it fell, and I tripped over my own feet before falling into the puddle of booze on the ground, as the painting tackled me. There was a loud gasp from the crowd, and then the room grew quiet. I lay there embarrassed like the fool I was. Three gallery attendants scrambled to pick up the painting from on top of me, quickly checking it for damage before rushing to hang it back on the wall.

As I attempted to stand up, I slipped again into the puddle of IPA. When I finally regained my footing, I stood up to find the entire room was staring at me with mouths agape.

I awkwardly grinned and pretended to wipe off my trench coat, which was wet and sticky from the booze.

"Fuck yeah, Johnny!" I heard D'Angelo's voice yell from an unknown corner of the room.

Four huge security guards quickly approached. They grabbed me by an arm or leg each, and carried me out the room and through the door as the crowd watched. When we got to the street, they began to swing my body, gaining momentum as I rocked up and down. They hurled my wet, noodly body through the cool evening wind. I landed on a pile of garbage bags near the curb. Laughter erupted from the cigarette smokers huddled outside.

What a grand entrance! And exit! Fuck me.

I stood up and attempted to brush the trash stench off of me. When I looked up, I saw Martin rushing out of the gallery toward me.

"Johnny! What the fuck! That was amazing!" Martin exclaimed. He ran over and hugged my soggy body before shaking me by the shoulder and pinching my cheek. "Now, Johnny, just because you don't like someone's art, doesn't give you the right to destroy their hard work on their special night!"

"Damn, man, I'm so embarrassed!" I said. "What the fuck just happened?"

"You really can do no wrong," Martin said. "Are you coming to the afterparty?"

"I really don't think they're going to want me to crash the after party," I said. "Not after that crash."

"Dmitry already left. He won't even know what happened. Trust me, you'll be alright with me."

After walking around SoHo for an hour, talking shit about Dmitry's show, and drinking more IPA from Martin's flask—we took a cab to an apartment building on Fifth Avenue. Across the street, Central Park loomed like a sleeping giant.

"We're here!" Martin said, motioning to the door like an obedient servant.

"Well, here we go," I said to Martin.

Martin grabbed me by the shoulders, straightened out the collar of my trench coat, smoothed the crumpled mass of my jacket sleeves, and gave me a playful slap on my cheek.

"Cheer up, kid," he said. "We're going to do fine. We'll be the belles of the ball." His gigantic grin was enough for the two of us.

I felt immense joy and pride to be hanging out with Martin as he rang the bell. The door unlocked with a buzz, and I walked in confidently with Martin Kippenberger at my side.

9

The bright lights of the foyer reflected off of the resin-soaked abstract paintings that hung on the wooden walls of the entryway. A security guard with an earpiece stood aloof behind a grand wooden desk. He looked skeptical as Martin and I approached, his gaze wandering to the door behind us, probably hoping we'd be headed back that way soon.

"Can I help you guys?" he asked in a tone that seemed reserved for lost stragglers.

Martin bowed and replied, "My esteemed colleague and I are here for the Dmitry Vaga afterparty. My name should be on the list. I'm Mr. Martin Kippenberger."

The security guard checked the list, holding it up close to his face like a myopic mole. "Alright, there you are, Mr. Kippenberger. And your friend here?"

Shit, here was the part where I got the boot.

"He's my plus one," Martin said.

"I'm only supposed to let people on the list up," the security guard said as politely as he could muster, playing nice now that he knew Martin was on the list.

"Well, my friend here has to be let up, kind sir." Martin reached inside his jacket, pulled out his flask, and passed it to the security guard. "Just take a drink, and you'll want to let us up."

The security guard rearranged his suit and raised an eyebrow. "Well, I am a bit dry." He took a gulp of the IPA, and almost vomited it up as he gagged.

"Jesus fucking Christ!" he said. He took a second to steady himself, and then drank deeply again.

It looked as though a spell had come over him. I could see the Tweety birds circling around his head. He looked like he was about to fall over. The security guard passed the flask to me, and I took a gulp.

"Damn, you guys are alright. Go on up. And if anyone asks, I didn't let you in." He pressed the elevator button for us.

The sparkly, golden elevator opened its doors to reveal a cream-colored, carpeted floor that looked like it'd never been stepped on.

"It's on floor 15, " the security guard said. "Mr. Rockefeller has the whole floor. Make a left out of the elevator, and that's it. Enjoy, boys." As the elevator doors closed, I got a good whiff of my trench coat. Fuck, I smelled like a dead wino brined in a vat of liquor.

"Woo boy, you smell like shit," Martin said. I wondered if he could read minds.

The party was decadent. There were many old, rich assholes in tuxedos and gowns talking among themselves and drinking champagne that waiters carried around on silver trays. Classical music wafted in the air above the quiet chatter of these elites. I felt underdressed for the occasion, but I didn't have any tuxedos laying around in my loft so I didn't really give a shit. I spotted plenty of artists in the crowd who looked just as confused as I was.

The architecture of the apartment was Art Deco, and the place looked like an interior decorator's wet dream, stuffed with rare mid-century modern furniture looking like it just arrived from a Knoll factory yesterday. A grand, baroque staircase led up to what must have been another floor of the massive apartment. The foyer itself was huge, and where most of the party concentrated. I tried to stick to the periphery of the crowd, but Martin walked right through a circle of aristocrats discussing Dmitry's genius show and I followed him. I felt out of place. Nobody else smelled like shit. Even the beautiful white marble floors were unimpressed by my old Converse sneakers, which squeaked loudly as I took in the stuffy, expensive environment.

I had crashed these types of parties before in my pursuit of selling paintings, but I didn't think I'd ever get used to being around these people. I was a hayseed that looked more like an unfortunate dust bowl okie than a prince of circumstance, probably a weird spectacle to these people who had been blessed by the lottery of being born into exceptionally prosperous families. The chosen ones eyed me curiously. I tried my best to appreciate the private museum. I felt more comfortable around the artworks on the walls than the people. I asked Martin if he knew whose place this was. He said he thought they were part of the Rockefeller dynasty.

The grand walls had a pantheon of modernist masterpieces hung tastefully. There were a few Picassos, a Braque, a Leger, an O'Keefe, a Kandinsky, two Pollocks, a Krasner, a few de Koonings, a Rothko, a Mitchell, a Twombly, a Frankenthaler, and the token wall of Warhols—and someone actually lived here.

When I finally finished cataloging the collection in my head, I looked up and realized Martin had disappeared.

A waiter walked by carrying champagne on a silver platter, so I lunged for a glass. He paused for a second and I remembered I still had my flask of IPA. I chugged the champagne down, put the empty glass on a table next to me, and took a sip from my flask. I probably didn't need any more booze, but I didn't think I'd be able to handle these pompous people without another dose of liquid courage. I looked down at the marble floors. The veins of the marble were dancing in a disorienting spectacle, grooving around, slinking, breathing life, caressing my dirty, white Chuck Taylors. I saw a door to a balcony and decided to step out for a cigarette. From the fifteenth-floor, I watched the treetops of Central Park sway in the wind, a beautiful dance of choreographed precision, the trees holding one another up to keep from falling to the ground. I tossed my cigarette in their direction and headed back inside to find more alcohol.

I looked around and saw Jacques and Dmitry talking in a corner. Jacques was wearing a blue velvet suit with a bright red ascot loudly announcing his presence. The Gesualdo-looking motherfucker had style, I had to give him that. Dmitry had on a black velvet turtleneck with a golden Chanel logo stitched above his left breast, white leather cargo pants, traffic cone orange Doc Martin boots. He looked like a confused rock star.

I grabbed two more glasses of champagne from a waiter and chugged one down. Jacques locked eyes with me and motioned for me to come over. I chugged the other glass down and mosied over in their direction.

"Johnnyeee!" Jacques squealed in delight. "The man everyone is talking about." I wondered if he was mocking me with his glee. "Do you know Dmitry?" Dmitry eyed me with disinterest.

"No, we haven't met yet. I'm Johnny Dabs," I said as we shook hands. "Congratulations on the show."

"Thanks," Dmitry said.

"Dmitry, you must know Johnny and his work. He's a painter,

and tonight he became a performance artist. Johnny's the one who knocked your painting off the wall at the opening." I wished Martin was there to deflect from my unfortunate spectacle.

"Oh, great, another artist," Dmitry said, enthusiasm flooding out of his mouth. "You certainly smell like an artist."

"Yeah, um, sorry about that," I said. "It was a great show though. Hey, I went to a party at your compound when I was in LA a few months ago. It was an interesting scene, very cool."

"I don't remember seeing you there, but I heard you met my friend Lada that night. She had nice things to say about you." A smug smile slowly formed on Dmitry's face.

The Russian woman's face cluttered my mind. "Oh, uh, Lada, yes." I felt exposed, embarrassed by my clumsy night with her, but I tried to play it off.

"I did see your show at Christian's in Cologne," Dmitry said. "Interesting work."

"Oh, cool. Glad you dug it." I said.

"Will you please excuse us, Dmitry," Jacques said. "Johnny and I have some things to discuss."

Dmitry looked at us with a bored expression on his face, said nothing, and walked away and into the adoring crowd.

"Now, Johnny," Jacques said. "I hope your studio situation isn't too much of an inconvenience. I just wanted you to know that everything is settled."

"Yeah, um, when are you going to swing by and pick up the boxes?" I asked.

"They'll be gone before you know it," Jacques said. "Also, and this is very important, you need to keep our little arrangement to yourself. This is strictly between us. Me and my associates won't be happy if we hear you've been running your mouth around town concerning our business dealings." Jacques glared at me and I saw evil lurking in his gaze.

"Sure, Jacques," I said. "I can keep my mouth shut. Have you seen Martin around?"

"Martin? Martin Kippenberger?"

"Yeah."

Jacques looked at me with confusion. "Martin certainly isn't here. I think he's in Cologne. Or Italy. Or Sao Paolo. Or L.A. I have no idea where he is, but he isn't here."

"Well, I came here with him."

"I haven't seen him here. But you've got a better idea where he is than I do," he said as he walked away, leaving me alone with my confusion.

The party was raging around me, but my drunkenness was waning. I decided champagne just wasn't strong enough so I took a few pulls of IPA from the flask. Then I figured I should probably drink the expensive booze provided by these rich assholes while I had the chance, so I wandered around searching for the bar.

As I explored the party from its edge, I noticed an open doorway and decided to poke my nose in. The room was a library. Empty, of course.

Inside the cozy room devoid of partiers, I immediately felt relaxed. I looked through the walls of bookshelves full of fiction, poetry, philosophy, history, anatomy, architecture, and art books. There seemed to be no logic to the organization of the books. Not one book looked like it'd ever been touched, let alone read.

I picked up a pristine copy of *Gravity's Rainbow*. I opened it and saw it was an autographed first edition, Viking Press, 1973, with a note by Pynchon himself, dedicated to some member of the Rockefeller family. It was one of those books I'd always wanted to read, but I knew it was a notoriously difficult novel. I was intrigued by the cover art, which depicted a yellow sunburst blooming in a reddish orange sky with "Gravity's Rainbow" written in a cerulean blue font. No one was looking, so I dropped the book into the inside pocket of my jacket. I figured I'd appreciate it more than whoever lived here.

I found the bar and ordered a gin martini. While I waited for my drink, I leaned my back against the bar and watched the curious social habits of these elite fuckers. I spotted a few artists I recognized putting their best charms to work as they tried to extract the interest of these bloodless stones. All around me, the hobnobbers were doing their desperate dance. But who was I to judge? I was there to do the same—I just didn't have the energy to work my charm.

I wondered where Martin had run off to. Did he just leave me stranded without saying goodbye?

As the party wound down, I circled the celebrators a few times looking for Martin but he was still nowhere to be found. Patting the book in my jacket pocket, I remembered my flask. I took it out for one last sip and got out of there as fast as I could.

I walked back toward my loft along the edge of Central Park in the chilly night. The streets here seemed quaint. I was so used to junkies and drug dealers harassing me on the Lower East Side that I felt like I was in Disneyland. My sense of comfort vanished when I heard the sound of footsteps behind me. Was I being followed? I slowed down as I approached a car gate leading into Central Park. It seemed to sing a song of refuge. I hopped over the gate stealthily, or as stealthily as a drunk man could.

I lit a cigarette, walked deeper into the shadows, and looked over my shoulder into the emptiness of the park's bushes. There was nothing but darkness. Wicked trees swayed sinisterly above me. I looked back in the direction I heard the footsteps coming from near the gate. A dark form of a man was walking toward me. His long trench coat seemed to be nothing but a shadow. Everything felt wrong. As the man got closer, I realized I was being shadowed—it was the demon detective from my loft, his blue skin appearing aglow in the darkness of the park. I couldn't make sense of his face, but I knew he wasn't Humphrey Bogart anymore.

"Hey, buddy," I said to him as he stopped a few feet away from me. His skin darkened to a shade of midnight blue, too dark to make out his face.

"Who are you now?" I asked. But he didn't answer. Instead he floated up into the trees and disappeared.

That was all. Nobody was following me, just some demonic entity haunting me.

I hailed a cab and went home feeling spooked.

10

The next morning, I woke fully clothed on the floor of my studio. As I stared at the ceiling, I remembered my clumsy and embarrassing night at the gallery. I couldn't believe so many of my friends had witnessed my possibly career-ending accident. They'd never let me live it down, although most of them probably thought I was a hero for bringing down one of Dmitry Vaga's terrible paintings. My mind raced, imagining the end of my career. Then I caught a whiff of the stench of the IPA sweating out of my skin. It smelled like the musk of death.

I rolled onto my side and realized something was different about my loft. All of the boxes of booze were gone. My heart dropped into my stomach as I realized my furniture was now arranged exactly as it had been before I became wrapped up in this IPA mess. My couch, fake Eames armchair, and coffee table were back in the middle of the front half of the loft. When I had gotten home last night I had drunk some more of the IPA, smoked weed, and poked around the boxes of booze.

Everything had been accounted for.

I felt violated. Who had been in my loft last night while I was asleep, and why hadn't I woken up? Normally, I was a light sleeper. I was pretty fucked up the night before, but moving all those boxes would have made a lot of noise and I didn't think I could have slept through it. I was totally baffled. I had wanted to be done with the boxes of booze, but not like this. My mind flooded with possibilities of what could've happened. Maybe I had been abducted by aliens. Maybe I had been secretly drugged. Or maybe there was more happening below the surface of my attempt to gain favor with Martin and help him out than I realized. Yeah, no shit, Marlowe. I got up and took a sip from the bottle of IPA to steady my hangover.

I felt a sense of danger strike my nerves like a thunderbolt as I remembered all the strange shit I'd been imagining lately. I thought I had been flying to the fucking opening last night, for God's sake. And what was up with Jacques? My gut reaction during my first encounter with him was to steer clear of him. Now I was wrapped up in this weird IPA mess. Why was Martin friends with him? The demon detective appeared floating above my bed. He looked like Arthur Rimbaud again as he looked beyond me and began convulsing in silent laughter. I had to leave my loft. The demon detective seemed like a bad omen now, and I felt compelled to get the fuck out of there, so I headed to get some food to soak up my nasty hangover.

As I rushed out the door, I collided with two impeccably dressed men who had been loitering in front of my building.

I hadn't gotten a good look at them before. They were both conventionally handsome. The taller one had jet black hair slicked back into a coif, dark brown eyes, a slender face accented by high cheekbones, and wore a smart black suit. The other was slightly shorter with brown hair parted on the side like Dale Cooper, and sported a stylish navy blue suit hanging tightly on his slender muscles

The two men puffed up their chests as though they were about to beat the shit out of me. We all stood our ground staring at one another.

"Watch it, buddy," the taller of the two said.

"Oh, shit, sorry. " I stammered back.

They both stepped to the side away from each other, then bowed while gesturing their arms toward the direction I was heading, clearing a path for me. I was taken aback because I thought they wanted to kick my ass, but I figured finance guys or real estate guys—or whatever they were—weren't known for beating the shit out of poor artists on the street. I'd never heard of anything like that.

"Sorry again, fellas," I said. "I'm having a weird morning. Sorry I ran into you, but I'm kind of in a hurry."

"Have a pleasant day," they replied in unison.

"Oh, ok, sure. Have a good one."

I walked away looking back at them, and tripped over some garbage cans causing the men to laugh like prep school bullies. I got back up, and walked quickly until I had rounded the corner. I peeked around the edge of the building and saw the two men were still standing in front of my door. They appeared to be conversing calmly with each other. I watched from the corner like a paranoid freak wearing a tin foil hat, feeling even more spied upon and violated than I had that morning. After a few minutes, the two men wandered off, talking and laughing as they turned down the Bowery.

What the fuck was happening? Were they waiting for me? Was I losing my mind? I fumbled for a cigarette in my trench coat, and felt my flask weighing heavily in my pocket. I took a swig of the hooch to calm my panicked nerves. Instantly, I felt my body relax. Then I noticed the weight of the book I had stolen the previous night. Pynchon, I needed to start reading it.

I headed to Dupin's Diner on Broadway for a greasy breakfast. It felt like every face I passed locked eyes with mine. Usually, most New Yorkers didn't pay attention to shit, but even the people across the street seemed to be taking a keen interest in me. I looked behind me to make sure nobody was tailing me. Then I caught a whiff of my IPA-soaked trench coat and realized how terrible I smelled. Maybe all the nosy pedestrians were smelling me more than looking at me.

At Dupin's Diner, I sat in a booth and ordered a Denver Omelet, hash browns, biscuits with gravy, and a coffee. I hoped a hearty meal and some caffeine would put my mind right. As I ate, I thought long and hard about Martin. He was so generous with his time, art, and money. He represented an ideal I longed to embody in my own life and career. He was a true cosmopolitan, constantly flying all over the world, staying in five-star hotels, partying with celebrities and royalty alike. But he also got into the weeds of every art scene, never letting some artist's provincial successes cloud his criticism. He called out bullshit when he saw it. If he thought your work was that of a charlatan, he was never afraid to let you know. I felt honored Martin liked my work enough to help sell my show out in Cologne, and seemed to take a liking to me as well. He was legitimately a renegade, an international bad boy of the art world. His work was so enigmatic and cerebral that many thought his success was nothing but bullshit. His critics thought he was simply a by-product of eighties yuppy excesses, and was more of a nuisance than a great artist. The whole *enfant terrible* act rubbed many people the wrong way. Especially if they were on the receiving end of his barbs.

Martin had been a heavy hitter in the art world for over two decades. His once thin body was now showing the wear and tear of his constant drinking. I saw it in his puffy, hungover face and jaundiced complexion. When I thought back to my nights wandering the city with Martin, it dawned on me how sickly he looked. Maybe I needed to stop drinking so much.

For now, though, I was thirsty. I dug into my jacket searching for my flask. I would cut back later when things weren't so chaotic. I took another swig and let the familiar warmth wash over me. My hands shook uncontrollably, sweat gathered in my palms, and I felt a deep panic coming on strong. I watched as the bland color of the formica table began to blur and animate. The table started slowly breathing and appeared to be a sentient being. A drop of gravy on the table looked like a seething pit straight out of a Hieronymous Bosch painting. I thought I could see microscopic demons dancing around the gravy. The sound of the sizzling of the grill had suddenly become a deafening roar as a waitress swung open the door to the kitchen carrying two plates of food.

"Magical," I said to myself as I watched the strange procession unfolding before me.

"What's that, hun?" the waitress said, snapping me out of my hallucination. Her heavily caked-on make-up looked like a frightening mask grinning down at me.

"Oh-uh-nothing, sorry."

"Ok, hun. You know," she leaned down maternally to me, "you can't drink alcohol in here. I understand though, I could use a drink myself."

I passed her the flask. She looked around to make sure nobody was paying attention and took a sip.

She quietly gasped and coughed. "Geez, that's some real hooch. I know it's none of my business, but you smell like shit."

"It's my jacket," I said. "I took a spill in some of this booze last night and haven't had time to wash it yet. My apologies."

I had a hard time eating since I was pretty hungover, but I did my best to get the food into my body. As I finished the rest of my meal, I looked out the window, and saw the German woman from Martin's studio walking by. I knew this was my chance to get some answers about what had happened last night. I jumped up, pulled out a wad of cash, and threw it on the table. As I began to take off in pursuit of the woman, I felt my shoe slip on the tiled floor. It felt as though I was levitating for a brief instant, my body perpendicular to the ground. I landed on my back. The waitress stared down at me.

"You alright, hun?" she asked, her mask morphing into a kind smile.

"I'm okay," I said. "Thanks for your service."

I hurried up off the floor and dashed out the door. I watched the woman's blonde locks bouncing further down Broadway, and ran faster to catch up, almost crashing into a taxi at an intersection. Pedestrians watched in disgust as I weaved in and around their commutes. By the time the woman turned the corner, I had almost caught up with her. I slowed down to catch my breath.

"Hey!" I cried out, trying to muster enough oxygen to raise my voice. She didn't seem to hear me. I approached her from behind, touched her elbow, and said, "Excuse me, mi . . ." She turned around, swinging her purse at my face like a trained assassin. I was once again on my tender ass and back.

"Fuck you, asshole!" she yelled. As she looked down at me on the ground, she seemed to recognize me. "Oh, I'm sorry. You're, you're . . ." She bent down to help me up.

"It's okay," I said as I got back to my feet. "I'm friends with Martin. I met you at his studio."

"Oh, yes, one of Martin's friends. You're an artist, no?" she said.

"Yeah, I'm an artist," I said. I felt my face heat up and realized I was blushing. An immense bashfulness disarmed me, and I stared at her with nothing to add. She was even more pretty than I remembered. She was wearing a long black leather jacket, black top, black jeans, and red high heels. The bag she'd hit me in the face with was a small quilted Chanel purse. I wanted to find out more about the beer vanishing last night, but I also wanted to find out more about her.

"All you artists are too wrapped up in your heads," she said. "What do you want?"

"Um, I just recognized you from Martin's studio. I had some questions about the beer being stored at my place. Have you seen him around recently?"

"I haven't seen him since the day I met you at his studio. I don't really know him very well, I just know he's a famous artist or something."

"I thought you were friends with Martin," I said. "Why was he helping you move all that beer?"

"I just see him from time to time when I'm working for Jacques," she said. My ears perked up at the mention of Jacques' name. "I don't know much about the beer. That's Jacques' business."

"Oh, Jacques, I met him in L.A." I said. "What does he do exactly?"

She gave me an annoyed look. "What I do, and what Jacques does, is none of your concern. Now please, I must be going." She sped up, attempting to exit the conversation and get rid of me and my prying questions. I followed. I knew I'd need to stall her if I wanted to glean any more information about Jacques' beer business. We were nearing an Irish sports bar that didn't look like the type of place I'd want to drink at, but it was convenient.

"Wait, hold up. Do you want to maybe get a drink with me?" I asked, and pointed to the bar.

"No, I don't think so. "

"Johnny?" a familiar voice asked.

I turned around and saw Elena walking toward us.

"Oh, hey Elena!" I said. "What are you doing here?" My face turned red again. I felt like a child caught with his hand in the cookie jar.

"Are you kidding me, dude?" Elena said. "My studio's on the next block. You've been there a million times."

"Oh, shit," I said. "I didn't realize where we were."

"I hope I'm not interrupting anything," Elena said, smiling at us.

"Oh, no, this is, uh, actually I never caught your name," I said to the German woman as she bolted away.

"Goodbye!" she said as she turned the corner, seemingly glad to be rid of me.

"What was that all about? You weren't hitting on that poor woman, were you?" Elena asked.

"No, I, uh, met her at Martin's studio and just ran into her on the street."

"Oh, yeah, you and Martin are inseparable now."

"No, not really," I said. "I mean, I have been randomly running into him a lot recently."

"Johnny, you smell like a rotten ashtray and a dirty-ass tub full of moonshine. Are you alright?"

"Yeah, I'm just a bit stressed, working on too many things at once. I fell asleep in my clothes last night and didn't change before I left the house to grab some food"

"I saw you at the opening," she said. "But didn't get to say hello before you got kicked out. You really stole the fucking show. Were you super wasted or something?"

"Oh, fuck, don't remind me," I said. "I got pushed by someone in the crowd and accidentally knocked the painting off the wall."

"I saw you at the after party, too. You looked pretty fucked up. Maybe you should lay off the bottle for a bit. I'm kind of worried about you. I think I saw you steal a book." She eyed me with suspicion.

"You saw that?" I asked.

"Yeah, I was about to go say hello and get away from the crowd for a bit, but these Swiss collectors started talking to me. We were right outside the library. We all saw it."

"I didn't think anyone would notice, but yeah I did."

"Well, people did. That was one of the Rockefeller's homes, and they've got cameras everywhere. You should be more careful."

I felt ashamed that people saw me stealing the book, but I was distracted by the departure of the German woman. I still didn't know her name. My sanity had certainly been waning. I tried my best to distract Elena from my descent into madness.

"Do you want to have a drink back at my place?" I asked. "Maybe check out some of these drawings I've been working on?"

"It's kind of early, but I could have a beer or something. I have to kill some time before I meet those Swiss collectors for an early dinner. Your place is close to the restaurant."

"Cool, let's go."

As we walked toward my place, Elena told me about a new series of paintings she was working on based off of the Aristophanes play *The Clouds*, but I was having a hard time keeping up with the conversation as my mind was wandering to the day's many strange events. The disappearing IPA. The two handsome men in front of my place. The magic gravy at the diner. The German woman. My millionth public fall. What was happening to me?

A breeze blew, and I looked sideways at Elena as a burst of sunlight illuminated her profile. I thought that Elena was perfect, and I kept watching her talk without listening to a word she said. I thought of the German woman for a split second, but she dropped from my thoughts as Elena glanced over at me and I stared into her intense green eyes. For the first time in our two year long friendship, I wondered whether I was actually in love with Elena. I'd never thought of her like that, but maybe I was hiding that truth from myself. Maybe I was ashamed of the possibility of having feelings for her because I knew she didn't feel the same way about me. I always considered her a friend, and galaxies away from me with her talent, brains, and beauty. My body felt heavy, my vision became blurry, and I realized I was wasted as shit.

"You ok?" Elena asked. "Are you drunk or something?"

"Maybe a little bit," I said.

"Jesus, Johnny! Are me and D'Anglelo going to have to stage an intervention? You can't keep drinking like this. It's only two o'clock."

"I know," I said. "I'll clean up, I promise. I've just been dealing with a lot of stressful shit."

When we reached my apartment, I put my key in the lock and tried to push the door open, but it stopped halfway. I leaned into it, but it wouldn't budge. Fuck, the pallets of booze were back in my loft. I glanced inside, and saw them piled there again.

"What's up?" Elena asked. She looked over my shoulder trying to see what the hold-up was.

Panicked, I had no clue how to proceed. I had no idea why the IPA was back in my loft, and an immense anxiety began to suffocate my thoughts. I couldn't tell anyone about the IPA. If Jacques found out, I would surely be in deep shit. I shut the door quickly, and turned around to block the doorway. My drunken mind was full of fog, and I felt like I was going to fall into Elena's arms. She gave me a look of sympathy, and I thought I was madly in love with her. I couldn't let myself believe it, but the reappearance of the IPA had me flustered. I stumbled forward, as my shoulders slumped downward with a woozy fluidity. My eyes were level with Elena's and I looked into her bemused gaze. In the heat of the moment, I grabbed Elena and kissed her like some impassioned hero from an old Hollywood noir film. She kissed me back for a second, then as she pushed me away forcefully into the door, I smelled the earthy scent of sandalwood flying from her hair.

"What the fuck, Johnny?" she said. "We're friends. I don't like you like that!"

"Uh-um-I didn't mean to do that. I'm sorry. I don't know what came over me," I stammered as Elena backed away from me.

"Seriously, what the fuck?" She looked at me with angry confusion and disappointment in her eyes.

"Elena, I'm so sorry," I said, as she ran down the stairs. "I didn't mean to . . ."

I followed Elena outside, but she sprinted down the block, only slowing down when she realized I wasn't chasing her. I let out a huge sigh and rubbed my eyes. I wanted to die in that instant. I looked across the street and saw the two finance guys from earlier were watching me with grins on their faces. Dmitry Vaga's exhibition posters flapped in the wind on the building behind them.

I glared at the men, went back into my building, and slammed the door behind me.

11

Three days later, my dumbass attempt to kiss Elena and the pallets of IPA had me feeling a persistent and overwhelming inertia that was weighing down every fiber of my being. It felt like the pallets of booze had me pinned down in submission to their alcoholic contents. I cleared some space in my loft to make more work, but the muse was nowhere to be found. I couldn't get Martin's studio out of my mind, and no matter how hard I tried to crank out some more paintings, my mind wouldn't settle down to make work.

Before I could get anything done, I had to try and find Martin's studio. Maybe talking to Martin about this IPA business would ease my mind and I'd be able to get back to my normal scheming, dreaming, and painting. Maybe Jacques—that outlandish Gesualdo-looking ghoul—would be there, and whatever bargain I'd gotten wrapped up in would be settled.

Despite feeling trapped and despondent, I got a call from the Los Angeles dealer saying he sold all of the work I'd shipped to him. Some big Hollywood collector bought everything. The dealer was excited and hoped I'd be able to ship out another batch of paintings. He had a few other clients inquiring about available work. I guessed my dwindling reputation in New York hadn't traveled all the way out west. Shit, I was starting to stack cash fast. I was living the dream.

The situation between me and Elena was something I desperately needed to confront. I felt too ashamed to call her but knew I had to be upfront and honest about my attempt to kiss her outside my door. I should've told her about my deal with Martin and Jacques, explained the situation with the boxes of IPA, but I was afraid of Jacques. He told me to keep my mouth shut, and he didn't seem like the type of person to cross. For some reason—even before I spoke with Jacques—I'd kept the boxes and money a secret, and hadn't told my friends about any of it. I thought that maybe deep down I knew I was wrapped up in some terrible bullshit.

I decided to retrace my footsteps with Martin on the fateful night that brought all this booze into my life. It had become nearly impossible for me to step out into the world without taking a large gulp from my flask, and I felt an intense craving for the IPA at every waking moment.

Around 7 pm, I stepped out onto Great Jones, pulled the flask from my freshly dry-cleaned trench coat, and took a giant swig. The street was mostly abandoned except for the familiar junkies, winos, and derelicts roaming around. My loft was the only sign of life on the little block. I lit a cigarette to prepare for my journey, inhaled deeply, and noticed the two financial squares I'd run into a few days ago loitering across the street. As we made eye contact, the two men waved a friendly greeting before ducking into a doorway and disappearing.

I couldn't understand why these men were hanging out on my street. They didn't seem to live on the block, and I couldn't fathom why they'd want to slum it with me and the rest of the degenerates that called Great Jones home. The Wall Street types were far away from their domain. Maybe they had major gentrification plans for my street. The streets of lower Manhattan had once been famous for the muggings, murders, and violent crimes of junkies and other desperate people, but since I'd moved to New York almost a decade ago, the shopping malls of global capitalism had moved in with a giant broom and quickly began to sweep away this contingent of humanity. Artists were moving out to Brooklyn to occupy warehouse buildings since the rent was cheaper. The bohemia of Manhattan was being forced out of sight to make room for the never-ending hoard of tourists and their checkbooks. A K-Mart even opened up on Astor Place, which had scandalized many of the artists I knew.

I began walking down the Bowery towards Chinatown as a cold wind whipped my back, my mind running through my hazy memories of that night with Martin, trying to remember landmarks and streets that could help me find his studio. All I could recall was the sweet, strange smell in the alley. Everything else was a blur. I had been too occupied with watching Martin's drunken antics to pay attention to my surroundings.

As I got closer to Chinatown, the sun melted into a night's sky. I turned on Kenmore to head down Elizabeth. The hustle of the work day had vanished, and people flocked to restaurants and bars, hopeful to erase their nine-to-fives from their memories. A Gingko tree swaying in the breeze stopped me in my tracks. As I looked closer at the tree, I saw its leaves morph into a salon of hundreds of visages moving in the chilly winds. They looked like Franz Xaver Messerschmidt's character heads, their faces brimming with every human emotion in a silent choir. I heard Gesualdo's arias in my mind and imagined a chorus of the faces melding their voices together, a primordial melody that every living thing has deep in its atomic makeup. The tree was more alive than the zombies stumbling around the streets. I stopped and watched the leaves for what must have been ten minutes before remembering my mission and hurrying away.

Familiar signs emerged, revealing the location I was seeking when I recognized an alley and took notice of the pastry shop on the corner. The veil of the mystery of Martin's studio opened fully, and I saw the steaming sewers, as the fragrant piss and shit infiltrated my nostrils, followed by the sugary smell of pastries. I walked to the door thinking it would be locked, but it opened easily, its hinges creaking loudly as I entered. Inside, I walked up the stairs slowly, taking every minute detail in through my eyeballs.

I walked up the first flight of stairs and, as I made my round up the second flight, a large man in a velour Adidas tracksuit and athletic shoes came running down the stairs. I tried to act natural, to pretend I wasn't trespassing. I stubbed my toe on the last stair as I took a step up, stumbled onto the landing, I rolled up in a ball, and crashed into the man, almost knocking him off his feet.

"You fucker!" the man said in a Russian accent. "Watch it, asshole!"

He reached into his jacket, pulled out a slim, black metal object, clicked a button causing a silver blade to pop out, and held the knife delicately at my neck.

I almost shit myself. "Whoa, sorry, mister!" I choked out in panic.

"Fucking idiot," he said, and snapped the blade back before continuing on his way down the stairs. I lay there in shock, completely motionless until I heard the door shut down below.

My heart was still beating violently when I approached the door on the fourth floor which was where I remembered Martin's studio having been. My palms began to sweat. I steadied myself on the landing, and took another sip from the flask.

Then I realized the door was already slightly ajar. I attempted to knock, but the door opened when I hit it.

"Um, HEEELLLLOOOOOOO?" I said into the room as I slowly inched my head through the threshold. The room was dark and empty. I lingered in the doorway as my eyes adjusted to the darkness within. I heard the sound of a door slamming above me followed by the sound of footsteps. I quietly hopped into Martin's studio to escape detection.

The room was pitch black with only a small band of light coming in through the cracked door. I listened as the footsteps softly tapped by on the fourth-floor landing and then fled down the stairwell. When my eyes had adjusted to the darkness, I saw that the empty room bore no trace of Martin's frenzied studio practice. The boxes of IPA were obviously back at my place, but all of Martin's paintings, crates of sculptures, his scraggly bed, and all signs of Martin's presence in the room were gone. I pulled out a cigarette and lit it, the flame illuminating more of the emptiness before me. There was some trash scattered about but otherwise the space was entirely cleaned out. I knew I wouldn't be finding any answer to the IPA mystery here.

Among a pile of trash in a corner, I noticed a stack of hotel stationary with drawings on them. I couldn't snatch them off the ground quick enough. There was stationary from everywhere Martin had traveled as an international art huckster and trickster: Hotel Grunwalderhof; Haus Westend; Ana Hotel, Tokyo; Four Seasons Biltmore, Santa Monica; Hotel Gravenstein, Ghent; Hotel Metropolis, Brussels; Hyatt Regency, St. Louis; Hotel Lutetia, Paris; Dolder Grand Hotel, Zurich; Omni Shoreham Hotel, Washington D.C.; Hotel Okura, Japan; Hotel Miyako, Japan; Akasana Tokyo Hotel. Each drawing was more detailed and colorful than the last. Some depicted blueprints for sculptures, others were sketches of installations and paintings he intended to create. As I looked through the stack of Martin's drawings, an immense joy squashed my initial bewilderment.

I stopped when I saw a portrait of Jacques. The drawing was masterful and clean. Martin's pen sketched the outline of Jacques' face fluidly and perfectly, no line out of place, no strand of slicked-back hair ignored. Crayon colored in the rest, color sculpted to form on the trashed paper.

I continued to look through the drawings in awe. There must have been around fifty of them in total. I paused at a cartoonish drawing of the German woman, recognizing her immediately. The sketch lacked the rigor of the portrait of Jacques's but Martin had captured her essence perfectly. I looked down and saw Martin had written her name beneath the sketch: Lola.

Lola was her name. The drawing brought her gorgeous face from the depths of my mind to my lonely heart, and I thought about Elena. I felt a deep shame and depression. A sound stirred from a corner of the room. I turned around and tried to locate the origin of the sound but saw nothing but the empty room.

I turned back to the stack of drawings. I had to keep them. Even if Martin had intended to throw them away, they deserved to be saved for posterity. I folded up the drawings and put them inside my trench coat pocket. Then I took out the flask and treated myself to a victory drink. I felt like a million bucks, and honestly the drawings might be worth that much someday.

As I walked towards the cracked door, it swung open and Jacques walked into the studio accompanied by three huge henchmen. Danger strangled my throat and I dove to the floor as if the filthy concrete might offer me refuge.

"Johnny, get off the fucking floor," Jacques said calmly.

"Oh-uh-hey, Jacques," I said, slowly gathering myself and standing up. "I was just seeing if Martin was here."

Jacques scratched his chin. "You can't be sniffing around here."

"Yeah-uh-well, the door was open so I sorta just let myself in."

The henchmen eyed me suspiciously. They all looked like linebackers in the NFL, each about six-foot-four and at least 300 pounds.

One spoke with a thick Russian accent, "This him, boss?" He rubbed his fist lustily, completely geared up to beat the shit out of me.

"Yes, this is our friend, Johnny. We weren't expecting you this evening. I'd like to introduce you to some of my friends."

I didn't know what to do, but I knew this was very, very bad. "I don't think introductions are necessary," I said, my voice cracking like a teenage boy's. "I didn't mean to intrude. I thought I might find Martin here. Is he around?"

"Martin's not here. This isn't his studio anymore. In fact, something tells me you won't be seeing Martin again," Jacques said, his tone increasingly threatening. "You shouldn't be poking around in other people's business."

They had me surrounded. The only way out was the window. I could maybe jump through it and hope to land in a dumpster four stories down, but I didn't like those odds. I was fucked.

"Listen, I don't want trouble. I just want to get in touch with Martin." I tried to smile, but realized my facial muscles had frozen with fear.

"Johnny, Johnny, Johnny," Jacques said, scolding me as though I was a child. "We removed the booze an hour ago, and you've become more of a liability than an asset. Please leave us the fuck alone or we'll have to take care of you."

I stood there silently, trying to find some words to diffuse the situation. All I knew was that things were taking a turn for the worst.

"Hey, man, I'm Martin's friend," I said. "I just wanted to help you all out. You paid me. You've got the booze back. I'll stay out of your hair and keep my fucking mouth shut. Honest."

"Hey, MAN!" Jacques said, mocking my voice. "You're such

a stupid piece of shit, Johnny."

He snorted out a laugh, then motioned with his hand by snapping his fingers. The three henchmen rushed toward me and I took off towards the window. I had almost made it when I felt a hand grab the neck of my trench coat. I squealed and put my hands up in surrender.

Murderous eyes descended upon me. Two of the men grabbed me by the collar of my trench coat, while the third pulled out a syringe, took the cap off, and jabbed the needle into my neck.

I felt a sensation of warmth travel down my leg as I pissed myself. The men dropped me to the floor, and I drifted into the deep darkness of sleep.

The demon detective was fleeing as I screamed and chased him into an abandoned building. The war zone made New York look like some forgotten, grand civilization from centuries ago. The once-towering buildings had crumbled into a wasteland. I saw the demon detective's jacket wrap around the corner of a staircase, and ran after him. I kept screaming and screaming until the shrillness of my cries wiped the landscape away. Now I was in the woods with vampires flying around. I felt the dread of fear when they noticed me. The vampires began to swirl around in the sky in an apocalyptic hellscape. Hundreds circled around like water circling a drain. I pulled a syringe out of my pocket and began injecting them in the neck like a crazed soldier on a battlefield. The vampires flew away and I saw Lola in the distance. Her golden hair shined in the night. Her dress slipped off as I approached her. She ran naked into my arms and we kissed passionately. As we pulled away from our embrace, I saw that it was Elena in my arms. She screamed and ran away into the forest. And then everything melted away.

12

I woke up tucked into bed naked and with a boner. Immediately, I remembered my dream starring Lola and Elena. The throbbing sensation in my erogenous zone guided my eyes to the tent I'd unwillingly pitched. I rolled over groggily and realized I was back in my apartment. Then I remembered the events of the previous night and jumped out of bed. I was freaked out, but I also needed to piss with a fury. I ran to the bathroom, tripping over some art supplies on my way and banging my knee on the floor. Fucking shit, I'd been spending too much time on the ground lately.

When I regained my footing, I noticed all the pallets of booze were gone. At least I thought so. After I had peed, I walked out of the bathroom into my now spacious loft. I vaguely remembered Jacques and the Russian henchmen, but when I tried to remember how I had ended up back at my loft, I could only recall a big black nothing—a void. Why was I naked? Did those creeps undress me as they put me to bed? I couldn't remember

a thing. I felt a pain in my neck, and remembered the injec-
tion. Shit. I ran back to the bathroom to look in the mirror.
Sure enough, there was a little bruise forming around the in-
jection site. It looked like a hickey.

I walked over to the painting of Martin I had hung above
my bed and gazed at it as it stared back at me in horror. Then
I remembered the stack of drawings. I looked for my jacket
and found it draped over one of my paintings that was leaning against the wall. I rifled through its pockets and discovered the stack of drawings was still where I'd stashed it in the
inside pocket.

I pulled out the drawings and flipped through them once
more. Fuck, they were so good. I couldn't believe Martin had
abandoned them. Or maybe Martin had become a victim of
Jacques' strange underworld. I had known Jacques was rotten
to the core the first time I saw him in LA. I mean, he looked
like the musical genius and murderer Gesualdo, and that
couldn't be a good thing. He was a slimy piece of shit. But I
did appreciate his sartorial stylings. It took a lot of confidence
to dress that ostentatiously.

I decided I needed a shower to wash away the mysteries of
the previous night. I felt filthy and violated. As the bathroom
filled with steam, I was reminded of the steamy alleyway outside of Martin's studio. I thought back to the stairway, the dark
room, Lola's face, Jacques, the giant Russian henchmen, and
the drawings on the hotel stationary.

What was I involved in? In hindsight, it seemed pretty fucking stupid to have taken such an enormous sum of money for
something as innocent as helping a friend store a shit ton of
boxes of booze. And the booze. I'd been seeing some crazy shit
since I'd been hitting the hooch so hard. What was in Kippenberger's beer? It reminded me of absinthe at times, its harsh
kick was like that of the green fairy. Other times, it seemed to

be the smoothest beer I'd ever tasted. I realized I had been having hallucinations like I was under the influence of a strange psychedelic. I had only taken LSD and mushrooms a few times, but I'd never really had any intense visions when I was tripping. That reminded me, I needed a fucking drink. I stepped out of the shower, dried off, and found the bottle of IPA..

While I drank, I wrapped up Martin's drawings for safe keeping. When I had finished wrapping up the drawings, I heard a sound like a thunderbolt coming from behind me. I turned around and saw the demon detective hovering above my bed. Once again, he looked like Rimbaud. I felt the need to say something, to arrive at some clarity involving his presence.

"Hey, asshole," I began. "What the fuck is your deal, you Rimbaud-looking motherfucker? Why are you here? Are you enjoying this? Are you some ghost pervert that gets off on watching people? What do you want from me?"

Immediately, I felt embarrassed by my anger. I liked the demon detective, and didn't want to be a dick. I wondered if he was Rimbaud's ghost sent from the underworld to watch over me and protect me from this IPA mystery. I felt honored that he was interested in me and wanted to haunt me. He hovered there indifferent to my queries. Then he faded away like the chimera he was, leaving me alone to put together the pieces of my disintegrating sanity.

13

A week after my run in with Jacques and his goons, Elena had a pop-up show at an old storefront in Greenwich Village. I knew I had to go, had to be supportive, had to apologize to her for my awkward and inappropriate behavior the last time I saw her. When I thought about my attempt to kiss Elena, I just wanted to roll into the fetal position and grab the bottle of IPA to suckle on until I passed out like a drunken baby.

I had never realized how much of a crush I had on Elena. I was always attracted to her physically, but was also enamored by her paintings, intellect, personality and drive to push her work. I always knew she was out of my league, so the thing that fucked me up about it was that I never had any intention of making a move on her. Besides, she was a great friend who was always willing to help me out. She constantly set up studio visits with collectors and dealers and was always enthused when I sold work to them. There was no way I'd be in the position in my career without her help. I worried my attempt to kiss her was going to sour the camaraderie we had.

What was my life becoming? These days, I was only sober for a few hours in the mornings. By lunchtime, I was already hitting the hooch. Fuck, I had to stop drinking so much. Hard drinking was something I stupidly idolized in the lives of my favorite artists, writers, and musicians, but the reality of walking around hungover every single goddamn day wasn't cool. I had felt like complete shit for the last few months. I had to get my mind right.

I'd spent the week making paintings while listening to my Gesualdo CD on repeat. I was finally able to shut out some of the white noise crackling in my brain and paint seriously. I painted the demon detective, imagined a story of him lost in a labyrinthine struggle deep in a dark city. He made an appearance in about ten new canvases. I painted a ham-fisted portrait of Jacques in bright colors, looking like a porn star.

I thought about calling up D'Angelo to see if he wanted to meet somewhere in the Village before Elena's opening, but I felt too embarrassed to pick up the phone. I didn't know if Elena had told anyone about what had happened. I worried Elena was upset with me, and I was afraid to face D'Angelo as well, fearing that she'd confided in him. Maybe I was making a big deal out of nothing. It was just an attempted kiss after all. I hoped some fresh air, and the rolling of my feet might ease my troubled mind.

I lit a cigarette as I stepped out on Great Jones, looked up at the hazy moon, and surveyed my street. A shadowy figure walked down the block toward the Bowery, then ducked into a doorway just at the edge of the block. Something seemed eerie about the scene, like a desolate question mark hanging in the sky. I guessed it was just my nerves acting up since I'd have to see Elena soon and hurried on my way to her show.

I craved a drink before I went to the opening. Maybe that

would help. I pulled my flask out, and gulped as I walked past MacDougal Street, feeling a bit deflated that the mayor was nowhere to be found.

The pop-up was on Bedford, and I slowed down as I neared the street. I could see an artsy-looking crowd gathered outside of Elena's show. No, I couldn't head there right away. I needed a real drink, a real drink from a bar to clear my head.

I heard a piano being played through a door that looked just shitty enough for me to enter. A neon sign flashed "S.Spades" in cerulean blue. My heart was full of the blues, so I figured fate was forcing me to check it out.

Inside, a middle-aged woman in a black cocktail dress on a stage draped in red velvet was playing a Thelonius Monk song and nodding her head absentmindedly to the beat. A sign on the edge of the piano stand read, "Argentina's Famous La Maga, Jazz Pianist to the Stars." I wondered where the stars were.

The bar was dead, just a few drunk sad sacks rudely indifferent to the sparkling sounds of the pianist, telling their tales to the bored bartender. I took a seat at a table in the corner and noticed an attractive woman in her forties walking to the bar wearing a leopard-print pillbox hat and a long camel-hair coat. I liked her style. I nursed a dirty martini, chasing it down with sneaky sips of IPA from my flask.

The dark red ambiance of the bar's interior relaxed me. I watched a candle's flame dance, becoming mesmerized by the flame as it moved to the beat of the piano. The candle melted onto the table, and then the table appeared to catch fire. The candle wax rematerialized, enveloping the table and causing the raging fire to extinguish. A skin grew, covering the wood and eliminating all trace of the fire. Next the skin grew tiny hairs all over and began to breathe. It was a bit confounding but I felt at ease in the cozy bar. I picked my martini glass up, chugged the rest down, and went to the bar to order another one.

The woman in the leopard-print pillbox hat had sat at my skin table. She smoked a cigarette held by a long ivory cigarette holder. She blew a cloud of smoke in my direction as I stood staring at her, interrupting the strange happenings on the table. Her dark eyes sparkled in the candlelight and her hair looked like thousands of black snakes.

"I'm Victoria," she said.

"Johnny," I said. "I was just sitting here. Mind if I join you?"

"Of course," she said. "I was waiting for you to come back."

I was intrigued by her outfit, and confused. I tried my best to focus on her face and ignore her Medusa hair and the table that kept morphing and melting.

"What are you up to tonight?" she asked.

"I was supposed to go to my friend's art show down the street," I said. "But I decided to stop here for a drink first. I've never been here before, but I like the vibe."

"Are you friends with Elena?" she asked.

"Yeah," I said. "We're really good friends, and I love her work. You know her?"

"Yes," she said. "An organization I work with owns a number of her paintings. I was going to buy one myself tonight, but it was already sold out before the show even opened. Are you an artist as well?"

"Yup," I said. "I mostly make paintings."

"I'd love to see your work sometime," she said. "We're always looking for new artists to collect." The whites of her eyes appeared to be gleaming orange as I stared into her pupils. I looked down at the table, which was still covered in tiny hairs and breathing. I wondered if the table was actually a Robert Gober sculpture.

"You're welcome to stop by my studio anytime," I said. "It's on Great Jones Schtweet." God, I was drunk as shit. I was slurring, and felt like I was liquifying before this mysterious woman.

"Want to have a drink at my place?" she asked as she pulled out a compact mirror and checked her makeup. "I've got an apartment across the street."

"Sure," I said. Damn. I wasn't used to this sort of luck. And, I might even be able to sell another painting.

As we headed across the street, I caught another glimpse of Elena's show. I could see the back of Elena's head through the storefront window. Her red hair seemed to smolder as she talked to some fancy-looking collector types. I guessed she wouldn't mind not seeing me tonight. Victoria dragged me by the arm up the stairs of her stoop across from the opening.

In Victoria's apartment, I watched a radiator belt out an intense, steamy heat as she made me a drink. Eleven minutes later, she was smoking in bed like an existential philosopher, pondering the meaning of life.

"You can stay here a while," she said as I sweatily got dressed.

"It's too hot in here. Besides, I wanna walk around tonight."

"Be careful out there. Don't catch a cold."

I wrote my phone number on a piece of paper.

"Give me a call if you want to do a studio visit, or have another drink," I said.

With that, I was back on Bedford feeling like the king of the world. The pop-up show had mostly died down, just a few drunken aesthetes were loitering outside the darkened storefront. Elena was nowhere to be seen. I was relieved I'd avoided seeing her.

Lately, I'd spent too much time cooped up in my studio worrying about the IPA and the mess I'd been dragged into, but tonight I felt happy to be alive. The Hudson River was calling my name, so I decided to head west and take a stroll along the pier.

As I watched the glistening water, I thought of Jacques. He could've killed me. I couldn't just ignore the fact that danger seemed to be lurking around every corner of my life. As my paranoia returned in full force, I heard a strange commotion near the water. When I looked at the water, I saw only an empty pier illuminated by the neon lights of the city shining on the choppy surface of the Hudson.

Nothing. There was nothing to be afraid of. I needed to move beyond the fear that had been overtaking me lately. I reached for the flask and took a sip of the elixir. Then I heard a car pull up behind me. I turned around and saw a black limousine idling at the curb about twenty feet away from me. The limo's door opened and two men jumped out and ran toward me.

"Hey, you little shit!" a Slavic voice yelled to me.

I didn't know what to do, so I took off running down the pier. I couldn't tell how much distance I had on those crazy motherfuckers. I saw a dumpster in a park and dove behind it. I couldn't catch my breath, and my heart seemed intent on jumping out of my chest. I peered around the corner of the dumpster, and watched one of the men run past. Good. Maybe I had escaped safely.

I sat behind the dumpster, waiting until I sensed I could safely return home. But, if those were Jacques' henchmen, then they'd know where to find me. I didn't have anywhere to go. I guessed I could rent a hotel room for the night. Maybe get a room at the Chelsea Hotel. I probably wasn't too far from it, but I couldn't place where I was, just hiding behind a dumpster by the Hudson River, gripped by fear and trembling.

The lights of the limo flooded the little park as it jumped the curb. I moved further behind the dumpster and looked back to the end of the pier to see if there was another place to hide. Nothing but the empty pier. I was trapped. I heard footsteps approaching as the two men walked toward the dumpster.

"Hey, look, I think I found a rat," a Russian man said.

Fuck.

14

They grabbed me by my coat, pulled me up light as a feather. They weren't the same henchmen from Martin's studio, but I knew they were Jacques' men. One punched me in the stomach. I fell to my knees gasping for air. They laughed like the madmen they were.

"Get up you little piece of shit," one of the Russians said. I tried to pull myself up, but I slipped on a garbage bag and fell back on my ass. One of the men grabbed me by my ear and pulled me up as I squeaked in pain like a hurt puppy. I rushed to gain my footing. The other man punched me in the face. Meanwhile, the limo waited nearby, its engine purring. Another punch, and I was on my ass again.

Defeated, I decided to lay there, curling into a ball on the concrete.

"Oh, are we playing too rough for the sensitive little artist bitch?" one said. I groaned on the ground, covering my head with my hands to soften their blows. I felt like I was going to faint.

The two men dragged me by the jacket to the car and threw me in the backseat.

Inside, Jacques was sitting patiently, dressed in a black tuxedo and long velvet jacket. Gesualdo's murderous smile beamed at me. The henchmen pushed me to the center seat and sat down on either side of me. I could taste blood in my mouth.

"Always a pleasure, Johnny," Jacques said. An apoplectic anger raged inside of me, pulsing through my veins.

I sat silently. What did I have to say, anyways?

"Drive," Jacques said through the partition to the driver. He rolled the window up. He was seated across from me in the limo. I noticed a television and fully stocked bar that took up the length of the left side of the interior. Jacques reached for a bottle of gin and began mixing a martini as the limo skated down West Street along the edge of the Hudson River. He poured himself a drink.

"Would you like a martini?" Jacques asked.

I glared at him. My face burned with pain.

One of the henchmen slapped me. "The man asked you a question. Have some fucking respect."

Jacques stared at me, seemingly amused by my beaten face.

"I'd rather have some of my own." I reached into my trench, and both men tackled me onto the floor of the limo. They pinned me down with their knees, my face pressed against Jacques' recently shined two-toned shoes.

"Fuck!" I screamed. "I'm just trying to pull out a flask. Relax!"

"Boys, let him get his flask," Jacques said quietly. "But first kiss my shoes, you little piggy."

Disgusted by the thought, but feeling there was no other sensible option, I kissed his shoes.

"That's better," Jacques said. He laughed as the men pulled me off the floor and threw me back into the center seat.

I pulled out the flask and tried to empty it into my guts.

"You no longer like a martini?" Jacques asked. "I guess it's hard to go back to martinis once you're hopped up on IPA."

I ignored Jacques' question, stared out the window, and tried to take stock of where we were headed. The limo raced east towards the heart of the East Village, then south toward Chinatown, zigging and zagging a circuitous route through the streets. I wondered if we were headed to Martin's old studio.

"Where are you taking me?" I asked. My face felt like it was swelling and growing larger by the second.

"You'll know when you need to know," Jacques said.

The limousine moved out of Chinatown and headed toward the Financial District. I could see water out the window. We seemed to be heading west, but then turned south again. Then the limo came to a stop at the edge of the Brooklyn Bridge. The men opened the doors and hopped out, but I stayed put.

"Get out," Jacques said.

I stepped out of the limo, and immediately saw a gun in one of the henchmen's hands.

Oh, fuck. Was I about to die? I didn't want to die. I didn't want to die over $20,000. I might've been willing to die for two million, but not twenty grand. Plus, I thought my life was probably worth more than twenty grand.

The men grabbed me by the shoulder and led me toward the bridge, Jacques following close behind. What the fuck were they planning to do to me? Throw me off the bridge? Fuck, the water looked cold. I didn't want to find out how cold it was. I knew I'd freeze immediately.

Usually there was pedestrian activity on the bridge, but tonight it seemed like there had been a zombie apocalypse. Not a soul stirred. We walked for about ten minutes without passing a single pedestrian or bicyclist. I looked across the bridge to Brooklyn. The wondrous lights burned across the river—shining signs of life in the borough—as proof that life wasn't just a fleeting hallucination. I couldn't believe this was happening to me. I stared over the bridge at all these human endeavors unfolding beyond the water while death waited for me somewhere on this bridge.

The gun in the henchman's hand reflected the light as we walked. With each step forward, I felt death brewing. All of my life's ambitions would remain unfulfilled. My art career would wash away with my body in the cold, dirty water. The wind roared intensely. Cold gathered on my ears and face and burned with the biting wind.

The men stopped about halfway between Manhattan and Brooklyn. Jacques whistled a tune I couldn't place. I didn't want to go like this. I didn't want to die because I'd befriended Martin Kippenberger. I realized now the twenty grand was nothing more than a cruel parting gift. The men grabbed me by the shoulders, but I protested by trying to lean all my weight back and shuffling my feet against the pull of their strength. They dragged me easily forward and threw me against the railing. I hit the cold steel with my chest, looked down at the waves crashing into the bridge's stone construction. The men turned me around, lifted me up and held me over the railing. I squirmed. I knew I should protest, say something sinister, but I couldn't speak. Fear strangled my vocal chords.

"Johnny, you've been a great help," Jacques said. He pulled out a cigar and a knife. He slowly cut the tip of the cigar, and lit it with his zippo. He left the flame dancing in the windy night as he walked toward me until the flame was below my chin. The warmth felt oddly comforting. He flipped the lighter closed, and placed it back in the pocket of his long velvet jacket. His stiff, perfectly ironed white shirt beamed pale in the dark of the night. He held the knife up to my neck.

"Geez, Jacques, you don't have to do this," I squealed.

"That's true. I don't," Jacques said, alcohol-soaked breath rising from his mouth like a cloud.

"Uh . . .l-l-listen-uh-Jacques . . . I don't know what's going on. I just wanted to be Martin's friend. I just want to sell paintings. I don't give two fucking fucks about whatever I'm wrapped up in. I just want to make paintings and be left alone," I said, but my protest fell on deaf ears. The henchmen slowly began to push me further over the bridge's railing. I felt my ass starting to slip back toward the water. Jacques pressed the knife into my neck with a smile on his face, and then took a step back. A great panic chaotically pumped in my chest and neck. There were a million thoughts flying around in my head, but it was nothing more than an abyss of horror, a blank terror consuming me.

The men pulled me back down onto the platform of the bridge, once again pushing me roughly against the railing. Jacques approached, the blade of his knife dull in the darkness. One of the henchmen brought his gun to my temple, holding it steady as my head trembled. Jacques lifted the knife's blade to my cheek with a grin.

"Can you keep your mouth shut, you little piece of shit?"

"Y-yeah, Jacques. I promise you won't hear a word from me."

He cut my cheek slowly with the blade. I felt the warmth of the blood oozing down my face.

"Don't worry, you sack of shit. We aren't going to kill you tonight. If I hear you talking about any of this, I will find you and fucking kill you."

"Ye-ye-yes, sir!" I said.

"You know what to do, boys," Jacques said. He turned and headed back down the bridge towards Manhattan, puffing his cigar.

The men proceeded to beat the shit out of me again. I spent most of my time on the ground, rolling around in the fetal position, receiving kicks and punches for I don't know how long.

It seemed to last for an eternity.

I came to when I was woken up by a nice young man riding his bike across the bridge to work.

"You alright, mister?" He asked.

I wasn't fucking alright. Not at all. But at least I was alive. I limped back toward Manhattan to hail a taxi home.

15

The taxi driver wasn't excited to see me when I dropped my battered body into the backseat of his cab. Dried blood had caked all over my beaten, puffy face, and my entire body ached with a fierceness I'd never felt before. I needed to see a doctor. Did I have a concussion? Had I broken a rib or two? I didn't know. I just knew I needed medical attention, but didn't have health insurance, couldn't afford it. I loved being an American.

I stared out the cab window at the busy streets of Manhattan teeming with life. Pedestrians hurried to some obligation, some job that kept them distracted from the wicked world of people like Jacques. How many of these fine specimens of humanity were familiar with the depth of despair and danger my life had become? I hoped none. The cabbie kept looking in the rearview mirror to study my misery with detached curiosity. I couldn't help but burn with embarrassment thinking about what a sorry state my face was in. The giant gash on my cheek had already crusted over, preparing to leave a scar that would tell the world who I was: a tough motherfucker not to be fucked with—or a dumb motherfucker who lost a knife fight because he didn't realize he was going to be involved in a knife fight in the first place. But, hey, at least I hadn't pissed myself.

As the cab pulled in front of my building, I pulled out some cash and asked the cabbie what I owed him.

"Don't worry about it, kid," the cabbie said. "You look like you could use a break."

I looked at the meter, and saw the fare was just under ten dollars. I pulled out a twenty and handed it to him. "Keep the change," I said and closed the door behind me.

The cab pulled away, and as I walked down the block to my door, I saw what appeared to be a drunken bum sleeping peacefully in front of my door. As I got closer, I looked more closely at the sleeping form. He appeared to be wrapped in a filthy blanket, but something seemed off about the bum's quiet slumber. I could smell a combination of piss, shit, and body odor baking mightily in the sun.

"Hey," I said to the drunk bum. He continued to sleep silently.

"Excuse me, sir?" I said. "Hey, you can't sleep here." I lightly nudged him with my toe to try to wake him, and his limp body fell supine, splayed out into the anatomical position. His eyes were open and lifeless. My heart jumped into my throat and I began to panic. What the fuck? I came home from a near death experience to find a dead man in front of my door?

I looked closer at the man's face and noticed there were black marker drawings all over it. On his right cheek was a cartoonish drawing of a dick and balls, a scribble of pubic hair on the base of the shaft. A speech bubble, piss bubble, or cum bubble emerged from the tip of the penis below his temple. Inside the bubble, scrawled across his forehead, was the word "MoMA."

What the fuck? I didn't know what to do. I stepped over the body, and ran up to my apartment and called the police.

"I'd like to report a dead body," I said into the phone as if in a dream. The 911 dispatcher began asking me a bunch of questions but the shock had clouded my ability to answer her queries. I gave her my address and hung up despite her telling me to stay on the line, and then went outside to wait for the police. I stood on the curb away from the dead man, lit a cigarette, and stared across the sidewalk at the dead bum.

I heard the sounds of laughter and footsteps approaching and turned around to see Eduardo and Pat Hearn walking my way. Holy shit! My studio visit with Pat Hearn was today. I'd totally forgotten about it.

Eduardo waved to me excitedly and I waved back, not sure what to say. I guessed my face and the dead body said enough. A police cruiser turned down the block from Laffayette and sped to the curb where the body lay. An ambulance followed close behind. Two uniformed officers jumped out when Eduardo and Pat were fifteen feet away.

"You the one that called this in?" a female officer asked.

"Yeah, I came home, and found him lying there," I said.

The officers put on gloves and began feeling for a pulse. "He's dead alright," an overweight officer pronounced. Pat and Eduardo had stopped about ten feet away.

"You alright, Johnny?" Eduardo asked, as he took in the scene before him. Pat looked disgusted. I guessed she could smell the rot of the corpse when she began to dry heave. Her jet black, shoulder length hair swayed violently as she wretched with disgust. I looked over at them, my face bright, bloody, and bruised in the sun.

"I don't think so," I said. "I have to reschedule. I just came home to this dead man in front of my studio."

The cops eyed me suspiciously. "You just came home to this? What happened to your face?" The fat officer asked.

"Uh-well-I got jumped last night," I said. "I woke up on the

Brooklyn Bridge."

"Johnny, we'll reschedule," Eduardo said. "It looks like you've got a lot to deal with." He leaned down to steady Pat while she dry heaved. He guided her by the shoulders back toward Lafayette, leaving me alone to deal with the cops and the dead man.

The female officer went to the cruiser, spoke into the radio to alert the homicide division to the dead body. I had a feeling I was completely and utterly fucked.

The interrogation room had an old metal table and four chairs. Three walls were made of dull, gray concrete bricks, with a full length mirror on the wall facing me. I sat staring at my face in what I assumed was a two-way mirror. After what seemed like hours, I got up and began to scrutinize the damage to my face.

Shit! If anyone thought I looked like death before, then they'd think I looked beyond the tomb now. The wound on my cheek was about two inches long and crustier than anything I'd ever seen. How cruel of Jacques to fuck my face up like this. He could count on me to mind my business, keep my mouth shut. I lifted up my shirt, got a whiff of my musty stench, and felt a burning pain echo throughout my body with every movement I made. There were red marks all over my torso that I knew would soon turn into dark, beautiful bruises. Why couldn't Jacques just let me be? I hadn't told anyone about our arrangement. I just wanted to live the life of a successful artist with some cash in my pocket to pursue my dreams. I just wanted a life like Martin Kippenberger—or my idealized idea of his life.

And where was Martin in all of this? How did such an insanely prolific artist have time to be wrapped up with Jacques and his underworld? Or maybe Martin was in the same position as me, except Jacques knew Martin was too powerful of a celebrity in the art world to touch. Me, on the other hand, I was a loser, a nobody with nothing at stake, completely disposable in the eyes of anyone worth a damn.

Something told me I might never see Martin again. Either I was too dangerous for him to be around, or I'd be murdered by the end of the week. Or thrown in jail for the murder of a wino who the world saw as even more disposable than I was.

I thought of the painting Martin had given me. The frightened self-portrait seemed a presentiment of the terror that was to come. The drawings on the hotel stationary flashed through my mind, the images stopping on the picture of Jacques drawn perfectly.

The door opened and I turned to see an overweight man with a mustache, a fat, flat cauliflower nose, and thinning white hair lock eyes with me as he entered the room.

"Mr. Dabs? Please take a seat." He pointed to the chair I'd been sitting in. He dropped a folder on the table as I took my seat.

I moved my chair up to sit comfortably and cleared my throat.

"I'm Detective Gesualdio of NYPD homicide." My heart dropped when he said his name. Gesualdo? "I just want to hear how you found the body, so start from the beginning."

My face burned red. "Detective Gesualdo? Gesualdo like the Italian composer?" I asked.

"It's Gesuald-i-o. I am Italian, but I don't know anything about any composers. Now, just tell me what happened in front of your place today."

"I came home and the man was lying there. I tried to speak to him, but I thought he was too drunk to wake up. I nudged him with my toe to wake him up so he'd move. He seemed beyond wasted. When he rolled over and I saw his open eyes, I realized he was dead. He also had some weird drawings on his face." The detective looked at me with no emotion.

"And what happened to you?" Detective Gesualdio asked. "You mean to tell me you came home looking like that? What happened to your face?"

"I was beaten up on the Brooklyn Bridge. I was beaten so badly that I passed out and woke up on the bridge and took a taxi home and discovered the dead man."

"Something's not adding up here, Johnny. You mean to tell me you came home from getting jumped, and then found a dead man? Don't you have a job?"

"Yeah. I'm an artist, so I don't really have to be anywhere. I make my own schedule and work from home."

"An artist? What does that mean?"

"It means I make paintings and people buy the paintings for a lot of money. I live off of it," I said. The detective looked unconvinced.

"And what does MoMA mean to you?" the detective asked.

"The Museum of Modern Art?" I said. "Or, maybe whoever drew on his face misspelled 'momma'?"

The door opened and another detective-looking motherfucker poked his head in. "Detective Gesualdio, can I please speak to you outside?" he asked.

Detective Gesualdio stood up. "Please excuse me, Mr. Dabs. I'll be back in a sec." He followed the other detective out of the room and closed the door.

Holy shit! What had I gotten myself into? I knew how it looked. My face wasn't doing me any favors. It felt like the gray walls were closing in on me. My head began to pound, and a wave of paranoia washed over me. I needed to take some deep breaths. I'd be fine. This was just protocol. There's no way they had any evidence against me. Especially since I didn't kill the man. Hobos and winos probably died while sleeping on the streets all the time. I was only here because I'd found the body. But I didn't want to have to talk anymore about getting jumped, didn't want to have to describe Jacques and all my strange run-ins with him recently. If Jacques found out I'd been talking to the cops, then he would definitely throw me off the fucking bridge, probably with a bullet through my head.

The door opened and Detective Gesualdio returned to the room. "Well, Mr. Dabs," he said. "It seems someone up high's looking after you. You're free to go."

I was so shocked that I felt like I had been glued to the interrogation chair. I couldn't move a muscle.

"Did you hear me? You're free to go. Now get out of here before I start asking you more questions."

I stood and shook the detective's hand. He looked nothing like Gesualdo. He slipped me his card and told me to give him a call if I thought of anything else. I put the card in my pocket, and hailed another cab back home to take a shower and wash away the misery that'd been consuming my life.

16

When I got back to my building, I couldn't believe it'd been less than twenty-four hours since I'd first left for Elena's pop-up show in the Village. I'd gotten drunk, gotten laid, gotten chased, gotten kidnapped, nearly gotten killed, and gotten interrogated by the homicide division of the NYPD, all in the span of twenty-four hours. I'd accomplished a lot. Oh, and I'd found my first dead body. Couldn't forget that accomplishment.

As I was unlocking the door to my apartment, I saw that there were shafts of light coming out of the crack under the door. I didn't remember leaving all the lights on. I stepped inside and noticed an unfamiliar smell, as though cologne was hanging in the air. Then I saw them—two men standing near my bed. They were the two handsome finance guys I'd been seeing on my block. I gasped.

"Mr. Dabs, please don't be alarmed," the taller of the two said.

"What the fuck?" I said. "What the fuck are you doing in

here? Who the fuck are you?" Fear gripped me. Who were these handsome asshole yuppies? Their perfectly tailored black suits lent them an air of authority. They looked like the typical handsome, rich white men I saw all over the city, especially in the Financial District, walking around and making money indiscriminately. I never cared what they did to make all that money, unless, of course, they wanted to finance my wayward life by buying some of my work.

"Mr. Dabs, please sit down," the shorter one said. "We need to speak with you concerning some of your recent activities." His perfectly combed and parted brown hair glittered like a diamond from the hair gel holding it all in place.

"What are you doing in my loft?" I said. "You can't just break into my home like this. Who the fuck do you think you are?" The men slowly walked toward where I still stood in the doorway.

The taller one cleared his throat. "We understand this is a bit of a shock. I'm Special Agent Tom Sandal. This is my partner, Agent Tom Schneider. We're CIA."

"CIA?" I said. "What the fuck are you talking about?"

"Our agency has been watching you for a long time. Now, if you could just sit down, we can explain ourselves," Sandal said and motioned toward the couch.

"Mr. Dabs," Schneider said. "You're in a lot of trouble. Your face already knows how much trouble. The dead body that was out front earlier knows how much trouble. Please sit down and hear us out."

"CIA? Do you have a warrant to break into my place? I mean, I have rights. I can call the cops on you." As the words came out of my mouth I realized how dumb and fucked I was.

"Calm down. We're CIA, you can't call the cops on us," Schneider reminded me. "We've been watching you for a number of years. You're in a lot of trouble, not just from Jacques. We could have you thrown in prison."

"But I haven't done shit! What do you think you've got on me?"

"Glad you asked," Schneider replied. "You've aided an international plot to overthrow the United States government. You know all that illegal contraband you stored here for a handsome fee?" The two CIA agents exchanged knowing glances. I was trapped.

"How do you know about that?" I asked. "I was just helping my friend Martin out. How is that illegal?"

"Right, Mr. Kippenberger," Schneider said. "Have you seen him recently?"

"What does Martin have to do with any of this?" I asked. "He's just a famous artist. I-I can't imagine he'd be wrapped up in anything as absurd as trying to overthrow the United States government."

"Kippenberger has been on our payroll for nearly twenty years," Sandal said. "We believe he's crossed over to the KGB or FSB, become a double agent. We don't know how he got wrapped up in this IPA business, but we suspect his money-grubbing ways got the best of him."

"Martin? The KGB? Wait, what's the FSB? This doesn't make any sense." Fuck, I was in over my head.

"Have you seen him recently?" Schneider asked. "Our sources haven't been able to locate him for a few weeks now. We'll get to explaining the various forces at work, but for now we need to locate Martin."

I had a hard time pinpointing exactly the last time I'd seen him. Had it been two weeks? A month? So much had happened that I could hardly keep track of the days.

"Well, let me think about it," I said. "I think it's been about a month, maybe two or three weeks since I've seen him. You all think he's missing?" I couldn't believe Martin was some secret

Russian agent. None of it made sense.

"Our sources haven't been able to locate him for over two weeks," Schneider said. "He helped us recruit you into the organization, but he's been AWOL since the night of Dmitry Vaga's show at Gagosian. You were the last person to see him that we know of."

"How does Martin have time to make his work?" I asked, fixated on the least important aspect of these revelations. "He works for the CIA? And you think he's become a double agent? Hold on, I think I'm going to need a goddamn drink."

I got up to grab the bottle of IPA and a glass, and sat back down.

"We wouldn't recommend you drink anymore of that," Sandal said as he stood and tried to take the bottle away.

"Back the fuck up!" I said, surprising myself. "I want a fucking drink, so I'm going to have a fucking drink." I chugged some down, the harshness cutting against my throat as I coughed.

"Mr. Dabs, do you know what you're drinking?" the Toms asked at the same time.

"It's an IPA, or something," I said. "I'd never heard of it before, but it's pretty damn good. And it fucking works."

"That IPA you're drinking," Sandal said, "was developed by the KGB right after the Second World War. It's half India Pale Hopped beer, forty-seven percent Laudanum, and three percent liquid LSD."

I spit out the sip I'd just taken. "Liquid LSD? You've got to be shitting me, you fucking assholes." Just then I saw the demon detective appear behind the Toms and it all made sense. All of the strange hallucinations I'd been having since I started drinking the IPA. I felt stupid for not putting it all together sooner. I thought I was just stressed, and the hallucinations were coming from anxious nerves.

"The KGB, which is now referred to as the FSB, initially developed their 'IPA' as a brainwashing and truth serum," Schneider said. "They've developed a highly organized system of distribution amongst bohemian intellectuals such as yourself. They believe if they can infiltrate the creative class, then they can use the arts and artists as a potent propaganda machine to destroy the liberties of all Americans. Our fight is for the soul and fate of every red-blooded American. We hope you have the capacity to realize how sinister the battle for artists' minds has become. The human mind is the most delicate of instruments, and the Soviets are still using brain-perversion techniques as one of their main weapons to confuse and corrupt artists. We need your help to stop them from destroying our country, our freedoms, and our civilization." Schneider paused at the sound of police sirens screaming outside.

What? I sat there baffled by the things they were telling me. The KGB? Brainwashing? LSD? The fucking Cold War? "What the fuck's Laudanum?" I asked.

"Laudanum is basically a tincture of opium," Sandal explained. "It's typically reddish-brown and extremely bitter, and contains almost all of the opium alkaloids, including morphine and codeine. It's some deadly stuff. The bitterness of the opium, mixed with the bitterness of the beer hops, complement each other splendidly, creating a smooth but harsh taste. The LSD has no taste, but its effects are dangerous."

"I guess that explains why I feel so relaxed whenever I drink this stuff, and why I've been seeing some strange things," I said. "But, this doesn't make any sense. Isn't this exactly what your organization experimented with in the fifties and sixties? MKUltra and all that? You found it doesn't work. You can't brainwash anyone. You can't erase memories. You can't create a Manchurian candidate. That was all just a fantasy, helped along by thriller writers. It doesn't work, right?"

"That won't stop the Russians from trying," Schneider replied.

"I don't follow this at all," I said. "It's 1997, the Wall fell. Isn't the threat of Communism fucking over with?"

"International Communism is still a ruthless and formidable enemy, especially in the creative sphere, where artists' docile minds are led astray by their little left-wing kiddie games," Schneider said. "The Soviets don't just want that place in the sun that lazy artists bask in, but the sun itself. Their objective is the world itself, and they'll stop at nothing to obtain it."

"And who's Jacques? I assume you saw what he did to me considering you've been following me."

"We saw everything. We're getting there," Sandal said. "Nikolai Granovsky, alias Jacques Debiurre, was the head of the artistic arm of the KGB, now the FSB. Although we're not entirely certain how deeply the Kremlin is involved with Jacques anymore, we do know they still provide funding to his organization. We believe a group of former KGB members led by Jacques have gone rogue and have now gotten deeply involved with other suspicious, political organizations in order to dismantle all aspects of American cultural hegemony. Jacques was a highly praised painter of Soviet realism in the seventies."

"Wait, so Jacques is an artist?" I asked.

"He was an artist, but we don't think he dabbles much these days," Sandal continued. "His work was seized by the Russian government in the mid-seventies because of a series of subversive Pop Art-influenced paintings, and he was expelled from Russia. We're not sure why, but probably something to do with dealing drugs, cocaine and heroin mostly. We just know they had some dirt on him. He resurfaced in Germany in the late seventies, renamed himself Jacques, and was busted dealing cocaine and heroin in Berlin. He's been floating around Europe since then, dealing drugs for the KGB until the Soviet collapse in 1991. Right now, we're not one hundred percent certain how involved the FSB is in this terrorist IPA plot, but we know Jacques hates American artists with a passion. It's this vendetta against the freedoms we enjoy here that have fueled his IPA business. He wants to destroy the creative freedoms of American artists, bringing the United States down with them."

"What the fuck are you talking about? What freedom do we have as artists here? The freedom to die from lack of health care? The freedom to starve to death working a low wage job while following your artistic dreams? It just sounds like a bunch of bullshit to me. What if I don't want to help you? I just want to sit around and make paintings. I don't want to be involved with some sort of culture war." I couldn't wrap my head around this absurdity. I was pissed.

The Toms looked at me bewildered and then looked at each other. They paced around the room pretending to look at my new paintings. The demon detective hovered nearby, looking annoyed at the intrusion.

"Well," Sandal began, "you don't really have a choice. Did you not receive $20,000 to store an illegal brainwashing drug? Did you not aid and abet an international terrorist organization, attempting to undermine our democracy and destroy the freedoms we hold so dear? It seems you did those things. You can either help us, and we can play nice and help your career along the way, or we can prosecute you for the crimes you've already committed. The choice is between federal prosecution and federal employment as an independent contractor working on behalf of the organization. If you don't want to play ball, then you'll spend the rest of your days in prison. What options does Johnny really have, Tom?"

Schneider looked at me like a poor prisoner. "At the end of the day, it looks like this is the end of your fun little carefree lifestyle. You can join us, become a freedom fighter, make your country proud, have steady employment, benefits, stock options, healthcare. Or, we can throw your commie ass in a jail cell. Maybe you can lead a reading group about *The Society of the Spectacle* in prison. I don't think you'd . . ."

The door burst open. I turned around startled and saw Eduardo crashing through the door.

"Sandal, Schneider," Eduardo said, trying to catch his breath. "They've found Martin. His body washed up in the East River, under the Brooklyn Bridge. Martin Kippenberger is dead."

17

Eduardo came in from the doorway and put his hand on my shoulder. "I'm sorry for your loss, Johnny," he said. "I see you've met agents Sandal and Schneider."

"Wait, Martin's dead?" I asked the room. I felt like the foundations of my life were shattered and were crumbling into rubble. I became nauseous and my heart sped up. I couldn't process what was happening.

Eduardo affectionately squeezed my shoulder. "Yes, he's dead," he said. "You're involved in something very serious–and very deadly. We've got a lot to talk to you about."

It took a couple of seconds to clear up the cognitive dissonance of seeing Eduardo there with two CIA agents. "You're CIA too, Eduardo?"

"We've been following you for a few years hoping to bring you into the organization," Eduardo said. "Martin, in particular, wanted to bring you into the fold. We believe you'd make a great asset."

"A great asshat, huh?" I said, but nobody laughed and an uncomfortable silence hung over our vigil. I didn't know why I tried to make a stupid joke, but nothing made sense to me. Martin was dead, and all my hopes and ambitions seemed to die along with him. An immense sadness welled up inside me, and I felt anger—anger at Jacques, anger at these spooks, anger at the ineffable world, and anger at myself for being such a fucking idiot.

"Now's not the time for humor, Johnny." one of the Toms said soberly. "This is beyond urgent. Operation MoMA is already underway."

"Operation MoMA? What's that? Is that why the dead wino had 'MoMA' written on his face?" I asked.

"We need you to cooperate, Johnny," Sandal said. "Once we have a commitment from you, we can explain everything."

"What about you, Eduardo?" I asked. "How did you get involved with the CIA?"

"I was recruited by the agency while getting my MFA from the Iowa Writers' Workshop," Eduardo said. "I'd already been questioning the left because of their blind support of Castro's regime. My family was persecuted mercilessly under his despotic leadership. I wanted to bring freedom to my people. I knew the grave importance of squashing communism and socialism. These dangerous philosophies have impeded freedom's progress throughout Latin America. My people suffered greatly under the brutal dictatorships of leftist military regimes. I believe it's my duty to bring freedom to my people. We're at a crucial stage, the end of history, and making communism fall forever is the final step in our crusade. We need your help to do that, Johnny."

I couldn't believe the propaganda Eduardo was spewing. Communism? Socialism? The end of history? Most of the people I knew in the art world weren't concerned with geopolitics. Of course, most of my artist friends were typical lefties, but most of us just wanted to make enough money to live off our work. The artists I hung out with weren't organizing. We weren't protesting. We weren't all that concerned with biting the hand that fed us so sparingly. The shit coming out of Eduardo's mouth seemed so overly dramatic, far-fetched, and just plain wrong.

"That sounds like a bunch of bullshit to me, Eduardo," I said. "I mean, haven't our shady imperialist policies in Latin America fucked things up even more than they've helped? I mean, imperial powers, especially the US, have stolen an insane amount of wealth and resources from the indigenous people for over 500 fucking years. We've dominated their political sphere by installing unpopular and shitty, brutal right-wing dictators in the place of democratically-elected, left-wing leaders. We're not fucking protecting the freedoms of the people. We're protecting the fucking assets of imperial interests, shitty corporations, and corrupt-as-fuck politicians."

"I don't agree with that," Eduardo said. "Where's this coming from?"

"I read *The Open Veins of Latin America* a few years ago."

"That's a hard book to find," Schneider said. "We've been trying to ban that book for years. It's not exactly an objective worldview."

"Sometimes a book finds you," I said.

Everyone stared at me like I was a huge asshole. An uncomfortable silence strangled the air in the room. We all looked at each other with contempt. I was outnumbered by these juice heads all hopped up on patriotism.

Sandal broke the silence. "We had reason to suspect you might be uncooperative. We knew there was a high probability you'd be a suppressive individual. We cataloged your library the first chance we got. You have a lot of radical leftist literature. And the fiction you consume has an enormous amount of subversive, revolutionary potential."

"They're just books," I said. "They're not a call to arms."

"You're completely delusional," Sandal said. "Do you believe you're some sort of revolutionary artist? Do you think what you do is subversive? Do you think your ideals can save you from Jacques and his KGB minions? Aren't you a capitalist, after all? You think selling paintings for thousands of dollars to wealthy elites makes you some sort of radical? Do you like those new, white Chuck Taylors you buy every time you step in a dirty puddle? Get with it, Johnny. You're a hack. You don't believe in any of this bullshit you read. Your life proves it. You've got too much Nietzsche on the brain. If you're not careful, you'll end up just like him, in an insane asylum, rocking in a chair as spittle trails down your beaten face."

"You're going to come at me with some bullshit about Nietzsche?" I said. "So what? I like to fucking read books. I'm fucking curious, so I read. I want a better life for myself so I can have the time to pursue my interests at my own goddamn leisure. The world we live in makes no fucking sense to me. Am I supposed to live in a commune up in the mountains because I believe my little ideals are something worth striving for? I was born into this shitty country, and I live in New York fucking City. It's expensive. It costs money to breathe the shitty, polluted air, to have a place to keep me warm. If there was another way to live, then maybe I'd fucking pursue that. But what way is there, out there, really? What do my goddamn paintings matter to a random person on the G train? What do my paintings matter to some starving child halfway across the world, some starving kid just outside my window? Nothing I ever do will matter to them."

"Nobody gives a shit about you and your obsessions, Johnny," Schneider said.

"I'm an artist," I said. "But I don't think art fucking matters all that much. I make things. If someone wants to pay me ridiculous sums of money to hang my painting in their shitty, overpriced living room, well, I don't see any issue with that. Does that clash with my ideals? Maybe, a little bit. But, what your organization represents to me is pretty morally reprehensible. I hate you fuckers. That's my American freedom at work. I'm free to despise you openly. So, fuck off."

The demon detective seemed impressed as he hovered, his arms crossed, above the bed listening to my rant.

"Wow, that was quite the diatribe, Johnny," Schneider said. "You're quite the philosopher. Where'd you go to college, a state school? What a great university system we have here, filling you up with romantic ideals, a bunch of pie-in-the-sky, hippie bullshit. Do you want to air your grievances so we can get it out of the way before we take you to federal prison on international espionage charges?"

"Oh, let me guess, CIA guys? You went to Harvard? Yale? Am I on the right track?" I asked.

"Well, one out of two ain't bad," Sandal said. "I'm Yale, and Schneider is Princeton. Eduardo, you went to Cambridge, correct?"

"Yes, I did."

"Wow, a lot of elites in the room," I said. "Great, I've never felt more safe in my life. I still don't really understand why you're here. I'm just an artist trying to make my way in the world. Politics don't really concern me other than knowing you're all full of shit. I have my ideals and things I believe in, but I've never wanted to change anyone's mind. I've never thought it was possible to change the world for the better. I figure it's best to agree to disagree and be civil in the process."

"That's the freedom we're trying to protect," Schneider said. "We have to neutralize Jacques and his cadre of former KGB members before they can further destabilize our country. If the IPA is distributed in mass to all of the cultural influencers in America, then Communism will prevail. Generations of young creatives—with that IPA doping them full of delusions, and Jacques and his cronies brainwashing them—will rise up and be unstoppable. Their work will be influenced by these evil communists and they'll do everything possible to cause trouble, to destroy the way of life we've so desperately fought to maintain. We have Hollywood mostly under control. There are a few Orson Welles types, driven by a psychotic desire to stir the pot, but most of Hollywood is so wrapped up in vanity that a little money and a taste of fame is enough to control them. You artists are less docile, less susceptible to our pleas for help. If only all creatives were as easy to control as actors, then we wouldn't have to be here. We have to stop Operation MoMA. We're going to need your help, Johnny. Will you join us?"

I sat there silently for a moment. "I don't get it," I said. "You think Jacques is going to do some Charles Manson shit, brainwash a bunch of artists to go murder a bunch of elites or something? That doesn't make any fucking sense at all."

"You don't know the evil we're dealing with, Johnny," Sandal said. "It might seem outlandish to you, but if you knew what we know, then you wouldn't be so perplexed. Life isn't all fun and games and playing around with paint. There's a war happening just under your nose, out there in the streets between us and very sinister men."

"Here's the deal, Johnny," Eduardo said. "We can help you. We just need to be certain that you can help us too. All we are asking for is your allegiance to your country. We must continue to fight for our freedoms as creative Americans. There's too much at stake to sit idly in our studios as the very foundations of our liberties are under attack."

"What are you going to do for me?" I asked.

"We can offer you a very comfortable life," Schneider said. "What you need to understand is how deeply our organization pulls the strings of the art world. Most of your favorite artists have worked with us their whole careers. What we did for them, we can just as easily do for you."

"What does that mean? What are you offering me?"

The Toms looked at me from across the room with a mixture of annoyance and anger.

"Do you like this loft?" Schneider asked. "We own this loft. You're here because we chose you. Bill Donovan, the man you made that sweet deal with to live here? He works for the organization. Martin chose you. Eduardo chose you. Do you like selling paintings? We bought them. All of them, every single one you've sold for the last two years. The group show at Pat Hearn? That's us working our magic for you. Your show in Cologne? I mean, really, did you think all this happened because of how great your work is? Nobody cares about your work, not one god damn person gives a fuck about what you do with your paintbrush. You're nothing without us. If you become an agent, pledge your life to our organization, we can make all of your wildest art dreams come true. We can offer you the security to pursue your passions without the fear of failure. We want to help you grow as an artist. First, we need you to help us penetrate Jacques' inner circle so we can arrest him and throw him in the gulag where he belongs."

"I'm just an artist," I said. "It seems you CIA men should have this all under control."

"You know the Abstract Expressionists?" Sandal asked.

"Of course."

"That was us," Schneider said, a grin forming on his face. "We created those paintings. We made them important. We put them in the museums. We curated the shows that made artists' careers. We bought the work. We bankrolled the dealers. We have vast resources at our disposal. We can turn you into an art star. All of the bullshit you do, going to openings, attempting to woo collectors, playing nice with your peers, you wouldn't have to do that anymore."

"So, you're saying the whole entire art world is a covert CIA operation?" My mind was blown.

"Basically, yes," Eduardo piped in.

"Not just visual art–all art?" I asked. "How deep is the CIA involved with culture at large?"

"We do all of it." Schneider's shit-eating grin widened. "Every book reviewed in *The New York Times*, every profile of a creative person in *The New Yorker*, that's us. *The Paris Review*? That's us. Black Mountain College? That's us. Everything sanctioned by the cultural gatekeepers was, and always will be, CIA. Our network spans across the United States. Every single major city has a vibrant art scene, and we make sure those that help us are rewarded very handsomely. You can be a part of this history, be rewarded for your help. Or we can throw you in prison."

"Why me? Why would you pick me?"

"We don't want to reveal too much of our hand," Sandal said. "But let's say you were the perfect target for this mission. We can explain it more to you if you come down to headquarters."

"You want me to come down to headquarters in New York?" I asked.

"No, we need you to come to our complex in Langley, Virginia." Schneider said.

"Virginia? Like, actual CIA headquarters?"

"We know that when you see our CIA studio complex everything will make a lot more sense. Please, just help us. Say yes," Sandal pleaded.

The CIA had a studio complex? I guess I had no choice but to check it out.

"Ok, fellas, I'll go to fucking Langley, under a few conditions."

"Certainly. What're your conditions?" Eduardo asked.

"First, I want more of this IPA for research purposes. Second, I want to fucking sleep. I assume you all are watching my place."

"That's true." Schneider said.

"Good, you've got no reason to expect me to run. I'm fucking exhausted. I just want a good night's sleep tonight, before my mind's shattered by any more revelations. Deal?"

"We can let you sleep, sure," Sandal said. "But we don't have much time. Jacques is heading full steam into Operation MoMA. Tom and I will come by tomorrow at 8 am sharp and take you to headquarters. No funny business. We have cameras recording you, men stationed all down the block. We're watching you, so anything you do will be held against you."

"Deal."

With that, I walked the CIA agents out my door. There was too much to think about but I was too exhausted to think. I got in bed around three am and went to sleep to escape the weird nightmare I'd been living.

18

The lobby of CIA headquarters was dimly lit with flickering fluorescent lights. The ceilings were tall with depressing, scuffed up white paint covering the walls. It looked more like the lobby of a small business in a nondescript industrial area than a hub for an international spook agency. The cheap vinyl flooring was faux marble and reeked so strongly of disinfectant that I could taste the cleanliness on my tongue. The room was mostly empty, but there were a few Comrade Toms lookalikes roaming around. Toward the back of the room, there was one large wooden table with an attractive blonde secretary sitting behind the counter on the phone. My heart stopped when I saw her, and I instinctively pulled a cigarette out of my pocket and began twirling it in my fingers like a lucky rabbit's foot, realizing that I was pretty drunk from drinking out of my flask during the car ride from New York. To the right of the secretary was a bronze sculpture of an eagle perched on a branch, and behind her desk, an American flag dangled from the tall ceiling.

"This is CIA headquarters?" I asked the Toms. "It's kind of a dump. I was expecting something a bit fancier."

"This is the arts complex," Schneider said. "It's a satellite building that's unconnected to the main office a few miles away."

My shoe slipped on something, and I began to fall back as my feet went flying out from under me. I thought of how stupid, pitiful fate had brought me here as I landed on my ass, banging my head on the ugly floor. The flask of IPA in my trench coat hit the ground, making a tinny sound that echoed softly through the mostly empty room. God fucking dammit.

"Jesus, Dabs," Sandal exclaimed. "Can you walk ten feet without falling on your ass?" I assumed it was a rhetorical question. I looked over at the beautiful secretary and tried to play it off, but she rolled her eyes at me. What a charmer I was.

The Toms led me past the secretary's desk to an intricately carved wooden door with a large golden doorknob where Schneider tapped a key fob to a sensor. The door slid open, stopping just before the doorknob, revealing a long, dingy hallway with barf-colored, worn-down carpet barely covering the concrete floor underneath. The fluorescent lights gave the walls of the corridor a diseased, yellow hue.

I followed the Toms down the hall until we reached another grand, wooden door. Once again, Schneider flashed his key fob and the door opened to a cozily lit room. It took my eyes a moment to adjust after coming from the blaring fluorescents lining the hall, but I soon saw this room had actual marble floors. Along the perimeter of the room, there were floor-to-ceiling bookcases full of thousands of books. The domed ceiling was decorated with intricate frescoes, depicting patriotic scenes of white men with powdered wigs and wooden teeth haggling and dickering, founding the country and its values. I spotted Washington crossing the Delaware, but I was bored by the beautiful and grand paintings. I wondered why the artist forgot to depict a scene of the white men slaughtering Native Americans.

Sandal clapped his hands twice, and the lights in the room slowly grew brighter. I felt like I was in the secret library of a strange, heretic bookworm straight out of a Huysmans novel, plus the patriotic bullshit, of course. Schneider sat down on one of the four brown leather couches in the center of the room and motioned for me to do the same. I sat down, and took another gulp of IPA. I knew I couldn't handle the reality of the situation without a little help from my flask.

"Tom and I work for the CIA gathering artistic intelligence," Sandal said, pulling a book from the nearby stacks. "We typically aren't involved with the training of assets, but we've been tasked by our superiors to fully train you for our counterinsurgency mission to sabotage Operation MoMA. For some reason, Jacques seems to have taken a liking to you."

"It didn't seem he liked me very much when he almost killed me on the Brooklyn Bridge," I said.

"We know it was a harrowing experience for you," Schneider said. "You're actually our only assumed asset that's survived your association with Jacques. We've lost five agents over the last year alone. We were frankly surprised you didn't share the same fate."

"So, what's the plan?" I asked. "How am I supposed to help you apprehend Jacques?"

Sandal adjusted his necktie. "So you're in?" he asked.

"Do I have any choice in the matter?" I asked.

Schneider laughed. "No, not really. If you don't help us, you can say goodbye to any semblance of an art career. What would be the point anyway? We have enough dirt on you to take you straight to federal prison. Nobody would even know you were gone."

"Well, shit, I guess I'm in," I said. I could feel the IPA working as I started wooing and cooing with warmth, melting into the couch.

The demon detective appeared from the bookcase facing me, once again looking like Rimbaud. He must have snuck into the car as we were leaving. At least I had a friend to comfort me.

Sandal looked relieved. "We're very pleased to have you. We'll make your dreams come true. First, we need to show you the studio complex, introduce you to your partner, and then we'll run through your benefits and stock options."

"Does this mean I'm finally going to have health care?" I asked. "I think I broke my rib when Jacques' henchmen beat the shit out of me."

"Of course," Schneider said. "We have a doctor on site. He'll give you a check up. You probably wouldn't be up and walking if you'd broken a rib. But, you'll see the doctor regardless, make sure you've got a clean bill of health."

"Well, let's go check out the studio complex," Sandal said.

The Toms rose to their feet and headed for the door. On our way out, Schneider stopped me by the door. "This is just one of the many libraries you'll have access to, for any research you might want to do," he said

"Cool," I said, and followed the Toms into the recesses of the CIA studio complex.

19

We walked through a labyrinth of grimy corridors and hall-
ways. The carpet was the same barf color everywhere we went.
I could hear the bright yellow fluorescent lights buzzing in my
ears, the sound of which had started to give me a headache.
The spooks came to a large roll-down garage door painted
matte gray. One of the Toms flashed his key fob, and the garage
door lifted to reveal a huge warehouse space with worn wood-
en floors that looked like they had been transplanted directly
from Jackson Pollock's studio. Black, gray, and white wet oil
paint was splattered willy-nilly across the floor, perfuming the
air. There were large stretched canvases stacked along one of
the walls ready to be painted. On the other side of the studio
there was a wall of paintings in progress. I immediately recognized the black-and-white palette in the many abstract and
text paintings.

"Christopher Wool?" I asked, surprised since I loved his
paintings so much. "He's CIA too?"

"Chris is a good friend to our organization," Schneider said. "He makes most of these himself, but we also have assistants that crank them out when he doesn't want to bother. He's usually open to our suggestions as well. You know his painting 'Apocalypse Now'?"

"I'm not sure," I said. "Which one is that?"

"It's the famous one," Schneider said. "You know it. It's a text painting that says 'SELL THE HOUSE SELL THE CAR SELL THE KIDS.' Agent Sandal came up with the text for that, and some assistants made it. Tom is very proud of that one."

"Cynicism sells, what can I say?" Sandal said, shrugging his shoulders. "We tried to get that into MoMA through our channels, but it was deemed too controversial by the acquisition board. It's been passed around by our collector network to increase its value, and in turn, to increase the value of all of Chris' work."

"Sounds sort of like insider trading on steroids," I replied. "So, the CIA orchestrates all these sales, moves the work around, creating even more value through your associates?"

"Exactly," Schneider said.

"Doesn't this shit go against the American principles of hard work, industriousness, and meritocracy?" I asked. "Isn't this just creative fascism? I mean, if only the artists the government selects are afforded success, then doesn't that completely contradict everything you're fighting for?"

"Maybe," Sandal began. "But what's important is that we champion even the least digestible artworks, like your work, for example, proving how free we are as a country. I mean, if we were being conservative, you wouldn't be here in the first place. Isn't that freedom enough for you?"

I gave him a death stare. "I guess, yeah, it's good for me. But is that good for art? Like capital-A Art?"

"Art is dead, Johnny," Schneider said. "Whatever stupid fucking romantic ideals you think you have are null and fucking void. Pull your head out of your shitty ass and wake the fuck up! We have a duty to protect our country from these evil communists! Were you thinking about art while Jacques slashed your face? Were you thinking about art while you were almost beaten to death by Eastern European thugs? There's too much at stake. Can't you see that? Or are you too fucking drunk to grasp that?"

"I said I'd help, so I will. But I don't like any of this shit at all. I want to be clear on that."

"Come on," Sandal said. "We'll show you some of the other artists on our roster."

The Toms walked back toward the dingy hallway while I stared at the Christopher Wool paintings on the wall. Did I hate his work now? I wasn't sure. But, it definitely made me question my own tastes, my own artist heroes, at least the American ones.

I followed the Toms to a second garage door.

"Are you ready to see our crowning achievement?" Sandal asked.

"Is that door made of gold?" I asked.

"One hundred percent solid gold," Schneider said.

I knew what was coming. Of course he was CIA. Of course he'd demanded a roll-up door made of gold. I was actually surprised my mind didn't jump there first.

"Look, if this is Jeff fucking Koons' studio, I don't really want to see it," I said.

"Oh, well, okay then. Is someone a little jealous?" Schneider asked. I got the impression the spooks thought I'd be impressed, but all I felt was bafflement battering around in my skull.

"No, it's not jealousy," I said. A yawn interrupted my train of thoughts, and I inhaled a mouthful of patchouli-scented air. The hippie smell made me shudder. Were they burning patchouli in Jeff Koons' studio? "Sorry, I'm tired. And hungry. I just want some food and to know the plan. How are we going to get Jacques? If that's the mission, I'd rather find out more about that."

"Fair enough, Johnny," Schneider said. "We can head back to the library and have the chef bring you some dinner. Then we can discuss the mission in further detail."

"Sounds good to me. You all lead the way," I said as I took another swig from the flask. The demon detective emerged through the golden door and then disappeared back into Jeff Koons' studio. I knew I'd be seeing the demon detective soon enough.

As the Toms led me back to the library, they listed the name of the artist whose studio was behind each door we passed; Cindy Sherman, Robert Longo, Richard Prince, Julian Schnabel, Robert Gober, George Condo, Sherrie Levine, Mike Kelley, Barbara Kruger, Cady Noland, Jenny Holzer, Raymond Pettibon, and many more. Apparently, if everything went according to plan with Jacques, I'd soon be joining them with a studio of my own.

I took sips from the flask of IPA as we walked and thought about how strange it was that behind each roll-up door we passed were these huge, immaculate artists' studios, but I hadn't seen a soul since we left the lobby. I guessed the studio assistants had all gone home, their work days complete. The fluorescent lights kept buzzing, threading through every receptor in my ear. It looked like the nasty walls contained a million microscopic viruses all dancing around the paint, slithering and sliding to and fro. I watched them melt and vibrate into the walls as we retraced our path back to the library. The show of dancing bacteria came to an abrupt halt when I walked straight into Schneider, his shoulder bumping into my mouth, and all the pain of my fucked-up face screamed at once.

"You really need to lay off that shit, Johnny," Schneider said. He reached for the flask in my hands. "I'm going to confiscate this. We have business to discuss. You can't be all stoned, drunk, and tripping while we prepare you for your mission."

I was seeing shapes come out of Schneider's mouth as he spoke. The LSD was hitting pretty hard. Maybe Schneider was right and I did need to lay off the IPA. I didn't protest when Schneider snatched the flask from my hands. As we approached the door to the library, the buzz of the lights was drowned out by the beautiful sounds of Glenn Gould playing Bach through the door. I wondered who'd put on a record while we were exploring the complex.

Sandal swiped the key fob effortlessly, and the door opened to the familiar library. As I followed the Toms inside, I caught a familiar scent—sandalwood.

I turned my head toward the perfumed air and saw Elena perusing the library's shelves. She turned toward me and we locked eyes.

20

"Don't run to hug each other," Sandal said with a knowing grin. "Johnny, we'd like to introduce you to your new partner, but you already know her. This is Special Agent Carlyn Carol."

"Holy shit," I said. "So no Elena anymore, huh?"

Her emerald eyes stared at me with professional curiosity. "Out in the field you'll still refer to me as Elena, but I'm Special Agent Carol. That's how people refer to me at the Agency."

The Toms seemed pleased by the awkward tension this new revelation had brought. Sandal went to one corner of the library, and grabbed a leather-bound book. Schneider gestured toward the couches, and we all sat down on our own couch. Sandal handed me the book he had been holding. "It's a menu," he explained. "Our chefs can make you whatever you want if you're hungry."

I perused the menu. Drinking the IPA on an empty stomach had done damage to my psyche. The LSD or Laudanum had created a strange vibration in my vision, and while I felt unusually relaxed, I was also famished. I just hoped the cooking here was more in line with the fancy library than the shitty hallway we had walked through to get here.

"A filet mignon and some mushrooms sounds great," I said. "And, a bottle of the house pinot noir."

"Sure thing," Schneider said. He walked to a hidden phone in a bureau and placed the order. "You'll have full access to our world-renowned chefs once you've finished your training. Your meal should be here soon."

My mouth began to salivate with the thought of food. "It's getting pretty late. Am I stuck here for the night?" I asked.

"You can catch a helicopter ride back with Agent Carol, once you've been briefed," Schneider said. "We'll have to get you in training tomorrow, in Manhattan. Have you ever wanted to know how to kill a man forty different ways with your bare hands?" His mischievous smile widened.

"Training? Kill a man?" I said. "I'm not much of a fighter."

The agents cracked up. "We're aware you're not much of a fighter," Sandal said. "We saw how useless you were defending yourself against Jacques' lackeys. We've got a lot of work to do. "

"Can I have my flask back?" I asked no one in particular. "I want some more IPA."

Agent Carol looked particularly disgusted. "No, Johnny," she said. "Have you ever considered you might have a serious drinking problem? This isn't a harmless beer. That IPA is a powerful mind-controlling serum. Even worse, you're probably addicted to the opiates in the IPA by now. You're going to have to drink regular alcohol from here on out."

All I wanted in that moment was a little more of the harsh buzz. I wasn't sure any normal sort of booze would take me where I wanted to go. "You promised me more of this IPA if I helped. If I'm working for you, I'm going to work my way. And that involves more of that shit." I even convinced myself with that.

"We'll give you your flask back, once you've been briefed," Sandal said. "Until then, you're going to have to just enjoy the fine wine coming with your dinner."

The door opened and a silver-haired butler in a tuxedo walked in pushing a rolling cart covered with a white cloth. He placed a silver serving tray on the table in front of me and removed its lid, revealing a steaming steak with sautéed mushrooms on the side. I shoveled the food into my mouth. It was the most delicious steak I'd ever tasted.

As I chewed, the butler opened the bottle of wine and poured me a taste, like I was at a fancy restaurant. I took a sip. It tasted like wine.

"All fine, Agent Dabs?" the butler asked.

"Ahwr, yawr, showre," I said, my mouth full of steak.

My new coworkers looked at me, apparently disgusted by my lack of etiquette.

"We might have to spend a day teaching you some table manners," Schneider said. "You know, you're going to be eating some very fine meals with important people. You can't eat like a hog in front of them."

I laughed, and swallowed another bite of steak. "I dress up really nice, honest," I said. "So, what's the deal? How do I fit into your master plan?"

"We need to trap Jacques," Agent Carol said. "There's a pop-up on the Upper East Side that Dmitry Vaga's putting on in a week. We're certain Jacques will be there. We need to get him back to your studio so we can apprehend him—dead or alive."

Fear flooded my insides. "Dead or alive?" I asked. "So Dmitry Vaga's with the Agency as well? You always seemed annoyed by him, Agent Carol."

"Dmitry is unaffiliated with the Agency," she said. "His family has deep ties to the KGB, but they're so wealthy he has no need to join our fight. His career is funded by his enormous wealth. You'll find that the only artists that are successful that aren't affiliated with the Agency are simply rich."

"So Dmitry is just friends with Jacques?" I asked. "What's their connection?"

"As far as we can tell, they're just friends," Agent Carol said. "It's not our business to interfere with Dmitry's life."

"Oh great, so Dmitry just gets to do his thing freely without having to be involved with international espionage," I said. "Now I really hate his work."

"In a certain sense," Sandal began, "the agency works on behalf of the wealthiest families in the country. We help protect their assets overseas from being seized by corrupt foreign governments. We help them prosper in a country where freedom is free."

"Sort of like when the Agency helped all of those Nazis come to America with their stolen wealth?" I asked. "You helped them settle in America and let them keep their loot. What was it called again, Operation Paperclip? The Nazi scientists and all that?"

"Complaining at every juncture about the Agency's history will get you nowhere but a jail cell," Schneider said. "We're trying to help you live a life of freedom and prosperity. Remember, you received funds from an international terrorist organization. You have no rights, except those we deem suitable to give you. Besides, don't you want to be James Bond sipping on martinis, saving your country from deadly threats?"

I mean, it did sound pretty cool. I really liked martinis.

"So, you want me to go to this pop-up show and somehow convince Jacques to come back to my place so you can arrest him? Can't you all just arrest him yourselves? Why do you need me?"

"Jacques seems to have sniffed out all of our other agents,"

Agent Carol explained. "He hasn't figured out I'm with the Agency as far as I can tell. For some reason, he seems to like you. Maybe it's your work, maybe it's something we can't quite put our finger on. But, he hasn't killed you yet. That means something, although we don't know what. The two of us can lure him to your place. Then we kill him."

"Now we're just killing him?" I asked. "I don't think I have it in me to snuff out a life like that. I'm not a fucking murderer. I'm an artist, for fuck's sake!" I headed for the bottle of pinot noir. My hands were shaking as I poured the wine to the top of the glass.

"There's no other way, Johnny," Agent Carol said. "Jacques doesn't deserve to rot in jail. He deserves to rot in hell." Her bright green eyes turned cold. "He's already murdered enough people to be considered a grave danger. You'll be next."

I couldn't argue with that.

"You'll be fine," Sandal said confidently. "After our one-week training course, you'll be prepared. There's no better training in the world. We have a vested interest in keeping you alive. That's all you need to know."

With that, they all rose at once.

"There's one last thing we have to show you before we let you go," said Schneider.

Good, I wanted to get the fuck out of there. I followed them down the musty hallway. The CIA goons walked with pep in their step. I hadn't seen them eat anything all day. I wondered if they only ate in private, if they ate at all. Maybe these monsters lived off the blood of innocent artists like me.

We approached a doorway and Agent Sandal flashed his key fob. We went down a staircase and entered through a door into another hallway. The overhead lights had a sterile blue tint to them. We reached another door. Schneider waved the key again.

We walked into a room in which the air smelled so strongly of cleaning products it felt as though I'd taken a shot of bleach to the back of my throat. I saw a wall of aluminum drawers with handles and realized we were inside of a morgue.

Agent Schneider opened one of the drawers, and Agent Sandal pulled back the sheet. Martin's corpse rested there like meat at a butcher's shop. His skin looked like a wash of watercolor, changing from light blue to dark blue in some areas, from yellow ochre to jaundiced in others. It reminded me of the demon detective's skin, but inert, dead. I could feel a wretch coming from my belly, rising up through my body, and coming out as a dry heave. I looked at my new coworkers and wondered how they could be so indifferent to Martin's dead body.

"Why's Martin here?" I asked.

Agent Carol gave me a compassionate look. "We had to perform an autopsy. Martin's body washed ashore after weeks of him being AWOL. The Agency wasn't sure what the cause of death was."

"So Jacques killed him?" I asked.

Agent Sandal covered Martin's body back up with the sheet, leaving only his face exposed.

"Martin had liver cancer," said Agent Carol. "All the booze did him in. But we have reason to believe he died in the presence of Jacques. We think they threw his body off the bridge to send us a message."

"Operation MoMA is running full speed ahead," Agent Schneider said. "Only you can help us stop them, Johnny. You can avenge Martin's death. We wanted you to see what you were up against."

There lay Martin's cold flesh. This was the only part of Martin I didn't want to emulate. I didn't look forward to a death like that. "I'm here to help," I said. "Let's kill these KGB fuckers."

The agents smiled. Sandal covered Martin's face back up,

and slid the drawer back into the wall.

Agent Carol led me to the roof of the compound where a helicopter was waiting on a landing pad. She walked toward the helicopter and got into the pilot's seat, motioned for me to follow, and then handed me a helmet and headset.

"Agent Carol?" I said.

"What?"

"I'm sorry I tried to kiss you," I said. "I was just flustered, and didn't want you to see all the pallets of booze stored at my place. They were gone when I left for the day, then when we headed back there, they were there again. I don't know how that happened. I mean, I'm very attracted to you, but I seriously have always valued our friendship. I normally wouldn't've done that, so I apologize. I feel really stupid and embarrassed, especially knowing what I know now."

"We don't need to speak of it ever again," she said. "I mean, this is my job, and now it's your job. Nothing is ever going to happen between us, especially if we continue working as partners. Besides, I don't date artists."

21

I tossed my third cigarette of the morning onto the sidewalk as I wandered toward the DoubleTree Hotel on 40th Street. It seemed an unlikely training site for the CIA, but that was where the Toms had told me to meet them. Despite it being so early in the morning, the sidewalks were already crowded with tourists who were likely on their way to Times Square to clog their faculties with spectacle. I walked past the entrance of the hotel since I had arrived a bit early, and headed toward an abandoned storefront that had once been a porno bookstore. I lit a cigarette outside the entrance and watched the happy tourists go by as I tried to get enough nicotine in my body to handle what I imagined would be a stressful day.

I flinched when I saw an arm reach over my shoulder, and I felt a bicep flexing against my neck before being pulled violently backwards. I squirmed, tried to fight it, but felt the immense muscles of my attacker, and tried to go with his violent flow. Shit, I'd gotten too used to being dragged around like a ragdoll.

Indifferent pedestrians streamed by, completely unconcerned or oblivious to the fact that I was currently being unwillingly yanked into an abandoned storefront. I loved New York.

The man dragged me inside, forcefully twirled me as I did a clumsy pirouette and crashed into an overturned trash can leaning against a wall. I smelled death. I finally got a look at him from the ground. He was a short, stout, swarthy man with a face that hadn't seen a razor for a few days. He looked like a troglodyte bodybuilder. I saw his ripped muscles underneath his long coat. I stood up, ready for whatever this buff fucker had to say. He charged me, pushed me against the wall with all his momentum, grabbed me by the belt buckle, lifted me up with one hand, and held me up against the wall. I saw his other hand reach into his coat and pull out a knife as I was getting a wedgie. His bloodshot eyes bulged, anger pumping through the veins.

"What th-the fuck, man!" I struggled in protest. He brought the knife to my slashed cheek. A gold tooth sparkled between his other coffee-stained teeth as a psychopathic smile slowly spread across his face. His breath smelled like a dumpster with some coffee thrown into it. He traced the knife's blade along my crusty wound in silence as my underwear and pants kept riding further and further up, strangling my balls.

"Keep your mouth shut, or I'll cut out your fucking tongue," he said with a Slavic accent. "Jacques says to keep your fucking mouth shut."

"Yeah, ok, go-got it," I said with the familiar, charming ease I'd become accustomed to when dealing with disturbed Russians. "Tell Jacques, I'm cool, man. I'm cool. He won't have any problems from me. Honest."

The tiny, buff man lowered me. As I felt my feet reach the floor, I pulled my underwear out of my ass crack, relief washing over me. Then the man punched me in the face a few times.

I lost my footing, fell to my side, and hit my head on the trash can. He kicked me a few times in the stomach as I tried to get up, a thoughtful parting gift from my new friend. I watched the little man hurry out the door, joining the throngs of tourists excitedly taking in the sights.

I waited on the floor for about five minutes to make sure the coast was clear, made a beeline back to the top floor of the DoubleTree, and found the Toms waiting on some couches just outside the elevators.

"You're late," Schneider said disappointed. "Don't ever be late again." I felt like a punished schoolboy.

"Yeah, sorry about that," I said, realizing the henchman hadn't calmed my nerves. "One of Jacques' men just dragged me into an abandoned porno shop, and had some things to tell me.."

"Just now? What'd he say?" Sandal said, surprised.

"He said, 'punch, punch'," I joked. "He had a message from Jacques to me: he said I should keep my fucking mouth shut, with a knife to my throat. Then he punched me again, and kicked me in the ribs a few times. If this is part of the training, you can both fuck right off. I don't appreciate having to deal with this bullshit."

"It's not part of the training," Schneider said. He looked to be solving some complicated theorem in the back of his mind. "We can't have you coming to the training site if Jacques' men are tailing you. Besides, we don't have much time. Jacques is moving full speed ahead with Operation MoMA. We have to cut your training short."

"We're just going to have to get started, see where we're at by the end of the day," Sandal said.

"Let's get started then," I said, and clapped my hands to prove how amped up I was. The Toms stood there staring like I'd embarrassed them.

I followed the Toms down a hall to a set of double doors. Sandal flashed the key fob. I followed them into the room. It was a full-court basketball gym, complete with bleachers on the opposite end of the room. I couldn't believe this giant basketball court was on the top floor of the hotel. There were wrestling mats covering the polished wood floors. I smelled sweat mixed with floor wax.

A man who looked like one of the Toms was on the court leading the training session. He had red hair combed into a greasy pompadour that didn't move as he turned toward us. We walked to the bleachers, my shoes squeaking like rats on the basketball court.

"Agent Sandal, Agent Schneider, nice of you to finally join us," the man with the pompadour said. "Please find a seat. You know the drill."

I climbed up the steps of the bleachers and looked around at my fellow CIA recruits. It was a motley crew of unimpressive-looking humans, about twenty of them. All were men who appeared to be in their twenties and thirties, with every race and creed represented, all looking like they drank too much. Along with the smells of the gym, I also sniffed a lot of hangovers in the air as I found a place amongst the outcasts. I wondered if any of them had also been exposed to the IPA. Everyone looked like a creative type, hip but grizzled by the effects of a life of boozing. I wondered whether this was actually an elaborate ploy orchestrated by the CIA to get me into rehab. It just made me crave another drink.

The man leading the training was Special Agent Tim Flanders. He was tall and lean, with a handsome face that was also tall and lean. His bright green eyes and red hair made him look like Christmas itself. I guessed he was probably in his late thirties or early forties. He wore a black official CIA tracksuit like an athlete in retirement.

I followed the rest of the recruits off the bleachers to the gym mats for a morning of drills, jumping jacks, and push-ups, before learning some self-defense strategies. They brought out a Judo expert who showed us some kicks, sweeps, and punches and then made us practice on the mats. I remembered a few of the Judo moves from a Yves Klein book I'd read, *The Spirit of Judo*, which was a great primer for the CIA training. When I read the book, I'd get drunk and practice some of the Judo moves in my loft. I should've remembered them when I was dealing with the onslaught of Russian minions that had recently invaded my life. After lunch, we spent an hour learning how to disarm assailants, and we ended the day learning various methods to kill an attacker.

"The simplest tools are often the most efficient means of assassination," Agent Flanders said. "A hammer, ax, wrench, screw driver, fire poker, kitchen knife, lamp, or anything hard, heavy, and handy will suffice. As you might imagine, striking certain parts of the body have more lethal effects than others. Puncture wounds of the body cavity may not be reliable unless the heart is reached. Absolute reliability is obtained by severing the spinal cord in the cervical region. A slit throat is efficient as well. And remember, no matter what sort of philosophical gymnastics your mind comes up with, murder is not morally justified. Persons who are morally squeamish should not attempt it. I suggest those cowards look beyond good and evil or get the fuck out of this business. The world isn't black and white. Our organization operates only within gray tones. But always remember that we are defending the world from evil, dangerous men. Murder may not be morally justified, but sometimes it's the only option we have."

I surprised myself by taking to the training rather easily. Some of the other recruits looked lost out there on the mats, but I unlocked some sort of hidden athleticism in my DNA. I felt proud and ready to kick the shit out of the next asshole with a knife that stepped to me. I could hardly believe it, but I was having fun out there.

The Toms spent the day watching me in silence. They were the only CIA handlers in the gym. All the other new agents were there solo. Throughout the day, I talked to a few of the recent recruits. It seemed all of them were somehow involved with the arts, and most of them were actors.

The person I felt most at ease with was a young actor whose career was starting to take off. He looked like Errol Flynn and even had a dim mustache hovering above his lips on his chiseled face. I was sure I'd seen him in an indie film I saw at Film Forum the year before. He was the most enthusiastic about becoming a CIA spook. He kept volunteering for the training exercises. They must've brainwashed him with a lot of James Bond talk. I liked his vibe, but couldn't get behind his patriotic sentiments. He was a typical actor—self-absorbed, vain, overly self confident—and treated every moment as a performance. I guessed I might've been that way too, if I looked like a young Errol Flynn.

The rest of the class made me and the Errol Flynn dummy look like legit agents of international espionage. I felt like I actually was a man of mystery, my trench coat disguising a man with frightening capabilities. I knew Jacques would've thrown them all off the bridge. It made me wonder what the agents that lost their lives to Jacques were like. Were they anything like these losers I was being forced to train with? If so, I figured I just might make it out of this mission alive.

When the training was over, the Toms brought me back to a conference room down the hall. We sat at a long, sleek, wooden table with ornate fleur de lis carved into its legs. A large abstract painting with a yellow background and two fuzzy rectangles stacked on top of each other—one red, one white—hung on the wall.

"Is that a Rothko?" I asked.

"Of course," Sandal said. "We have to enjoy our vast art collection somehow."

"We'll have to put you into the field ASAP," Schneider began, eager to move on from my moment of art appreciation. "We hope this minimal training will be sufficient. As you saw, compared to some of our new recruits, you're going to have a bright career ahead of you."

"Thanks," I said. "When are we going to go after Jacques?"

"We need you to lay low in your studio for the next few days since you were probably tailed here by Jacques' associate," Schneider said. "We don't think Jacques knows you're working with us, but we can't have his men following you here. Agent Carol will swing by your place, and you'll begin the mission per her instructions. We must warn you, our surveillance of your loft has been downgraded. We're still watching your movements but have to move some muscle around to gather more intel on Jacques and a few of his men. You'll have to put your training to use until the mission is over."

"Ok, fair enough," I said, resigned to my fate as an ass-kicker. "So when should I expect Agent Carol?"

"Before Friday evening," Sandal said. "Dmitry Vaga is having a pop-up exhibition of new work on the Upper East Side that night. We know Jacques is involved in the space that's hosting it. You and Agent Carol will go to the opening and after party together and try to lure Jacques back to your place. We believe he has a new batch of the IPA that's twice as strong as your batch. He's looking for a place to hide it. We think you might be just the man he's looking for. Agent Carol will further brief you before opening night. We've got another trick up our sleeve to convince him to go back to your studio that evening."

The whole scenario seemed outlandish to me. I hoped these

assholes knew what they were talking about. I was pretty sick of getting the shit beaten out of me, but being on my own didn't scare me all that much. Besides, these assholes hadn't stopped anything from happening to me even when they were watching me. I was ready to get back home. I wondered how long I had to relax before everything went down. I had a group show with Pat Hearn, after all. That was supposed to be my big break. Even though I'd learned that all of these opportunities had been orchestrated by invisible hands controlling my fate—which was why it didn't matter that a dead bum ruined my studio visit with Pat—I still couldn't shake my work ethic.

But I still had some questions gnawing at me. "Ok, I'm down, but I've got two questions: Is there like an HR person for me to speak to about health insurance? And, do I get a weapon, something to defend myself with? A gun, a knife, or something?."

The Toms looked at me like the idiot I was, then looked at each other and burst out laughing. "We're CIA," Schneider said. "We have your information. You'll get your insurance card in the mail, in no less than two days. And no, we can't give you a gun. You haven't been properly trained. Sandal, you got a knife for Johnny?"

Sandal reached into his pocket and handed me a switchblade. "Be careful with it. I just had it sharpened," Sandal said.

I flipped it open, stared at the sharp blade, and felt ready to put it to use. I bid adieu to the Toms feeling pretty confident after my day of training. I hoped I wouldn't need to kill anybody. I guessed my life's obsession with my career was borderline narcissistic, but I didn't think I was suffering from narcissistic personality disorder. I wasn't a psychopath after all. At least I'd never thought of myself in those terms.

22

When I got back to my loft, I hit the bottle of IPA immediately. I had initially felt invigorated by the training, but when I arrived home I felt a major depressive episode come on. I drank and stared at Martin's self-portrait, letting the heat from the hooch trickle through my body. As I looked at the painting, I watched Martin's face begin to morph and change into a million veils of pain. The painting breathed, inhaling and exhaling in front of my eyes. The edges of the canvas throbbed as the painting's subject transmogrified into a breathing being confined within the canvas itself. Martin began a rhythmic dance, his hands still shackled by the beer. His tortured face beckoned me to approach. I walked up and gave Martin a kiss on his painted lips. A loud crash snapped me out of the vision. I turned around quickly but saw nothing had been disturbed. The demon detective emerged from the shadows, and slowly floated my way. I paid him no mind, but I was glad he was there with me. He'd become a friend. It was a shame he wasn't much of a talker because I was curious about what his whole deal was.

I decided I needed some fresh air and food to clear my head. I took a few more pulls from the bottle and hit the streets.

Getting out of the loft made me feel better almost instantly, and the visions subsided as I headed north up Broadway. I decided to get some pizza, maybe end up at Last Bacall for a night cap. Night descended quickly and a brisk breeze made me tie up the belt of my trench coat. I felt the stares of pedestrians on the street and remembered the crusty scar on my cheek and my blackened and bruised eyes.

I stopped at a pizza place to warm up and grab a slice. As I stood at the counter eating, I watched the crowds of people stream by outside. I saw a man nervously smoking a cigarette, looking antsy and a little too much like a Russian ruffian. I knew he was waiting for me. If he was a tail, then he was pretty shitty at his job. I figured I'd have to lose this creep. I didn't have the energy to deal with another beating from a psychotic Russian thug.

When the man turned his back, I dashed out of the pizza place, leaving my trash behind like an asshole to lose the man. I sprinted to the street corner opposite him, looked over my shoulder as I turned down 8th, and got a glimpse of him chasing me. Shit. Twice in a day?

I ran faster with no idea where I was headed. I just knew I needed to lose this asshole as quickly as possible. I ran down St. Mark's Place, hoping I could duck into a business to evade my pursuer, but the sidewalk was too crowded. No place seemed like a refuge, so I began running in the street against traffic.

I kept running like an escaped convict, saw an opening in upcoming traffic, crossed the street, came to another corner, and rounded it. I saw a bar on the corner of 2nd Avenue and 7th, and ran towards it only to see another man in a trench coat running toward me. Fuck. I was trapped. I noticed a building under construction with its front door slightly ajar and dashed toward it.

Inside the half-gutted building, I ran down a hallway into a large, empty room with one flickering fluorescent light dangling from a cord in the corner. I moved towards the first door I saw and tried to open it. Locked. I tried another door, knowing the men following me were closing in. Locked. I was trapped in the empty building. Behind me, the men both slowed to a trot and laughed haughtily at my hopeless situation.

I turned around and got a better look at the two men. One was tall and thin with jet black hair and a mustache. The other was short and chubby with long, reddish brown hair down to the shoulder of his trench coat and a five o'clock shadow. The red head pulled a knife. I braced myself for a fight. What was I supposed to do in this situation again? Yves Klein's judo?

"There's no place to run, you little shit," the tall, dark-haired man said in a Russian accent.

"So, uh, let me guess, Jacques wants to tell me something?" I said as fear flooded my frontal lobe. Fuck, I'd forgotten all my self-defense training from earlier that morning.

"Shut your fucking face," the redhead said with a grimace and an accent that I assumed was also Russian.

"Listen, Raskolnikov," I began to blabber. "I don't know what you want. I'm keeping my fucking mouth shut. Leave me the fuck alone! I just want to have a damn drink, for fuck's sake!" I backed away from them and my ass hit a wall. The men seethed with anger as they assumed their positions to beat the shit out of me.

I felt the training seeping out of me as my instincts forced me into action. I lunged toward the redhead who was holding his knife, raised my hand into a karate chop, swung at his neck, and hit his throat. The man choked and his knife dropped to the ground.

The tall man came at me next. I ducked, swept my leg in front of his feet, and sent him crashing head first into the wall behind me. He rolled and pulled a gun out of his jacket and fumbled with it but I jumped and landed on his hand. I stomped on his hand and tried to ground his fingers into the concrete. I jumped again and this time landed on his face, the sole of my Converse crushing his nose. He screamed in agony as I began kicking him in the head with abandon. I kicked the gun to the opposite side of the room.

The redhead scrambled to his feet and grabbed his knife off the floor. He charged toward me, but I swiftly dodged him with judo ease, throwing him down face first onto his partner. I jumped on the hand holding the blade, and the redhead squealed and dropped the knife. He struggled to get to his feet but tripped over his partner's legs. I kicked him in the head again and again.

He seemed down for the count so I kicked the tall man in the head a few more times. Even though it wasn't brought up in my CIA training, I began kicking him in the nuts. I did the same to the redhead.

They moaned on the dusty concrete floor. I gathered the knife off the ground and turned toward the taller man. He looked up with blood spurting out of his mouth. He coughed, spitting a mist of blood up into my face.

"You got blood on me, you fucker!" I screamed. Something inside of me snapped as I looked down at the blood on my trench coat. I looked at the man and kicked him in the head again. I leaned down, put my knee to his chest, took the knife in my hand, and slit his throat. Blood gurgled out of his neck and he sputtered a bloody cough. He gasped for breath and looked up into my eyes as a dead stare overcame him and a shiver ran through his body.

I got up and stepped over to the red head, kicking him in the balls again. I looked at the bloody knife in my hand. The dark, rich blood looked black as death in the gloomy room. I bent down and cut his throat like a cold-blooded killer.

I stood up and looked down at the two men laying lifeless a few feet apart. Fuck, I just killed two men. I began to feel dizzy as a million butterflies flew madly in my guts. I swayed woozily, my body pumping with adrenaline. I went and peeked my head out of the building's front door to the street where pedestrians walked idly through the night, completely oblivious to the two murders that had just occurred inside the building.

I took a deep breath, walked back to the room, and tried to calm myself, but I was a fucking murderer. I dropped the bloody knife to the ground and kicked it toward the dead men. I knew I should scrub the blade clean to get rid of my fingerprints, but I was ready to get out of there. I figured the CIA would cover for me.

When I got to the street, I lit a cigarette. I could feel the blood drying on my face into a sticky reminder of what had happened only minutes earlier. I unbuttoned my trench coat and wiped my face with the inside of my coat. God fucking dammit. My favorite trench coat had the blood of two dead men on it. How was I supposed to get a blood stain out? I guessed I could afford to buy a new trench coat with my CIA salary. Maybe a fancy Burberry one in a darker color to better hide blood stains.

I just murdered two men.

I joined the unknowing pedestrians on the street. I knew I had to get out of the area. After walking a few blocks down Second Avenue, I saw a blushing pink neon sign that read "BAR" so I headed inside for a drink. A bouncer stood inside the entrance. I reached for my ID, but he raised his hand to stop me. "Go on in," he said. "You look like you could use a drink."

The bar was dark and dank and had the feeling of an underground cavern. Billie Holiday's "Easy Living" played on the jukebox. About five patrons crowded the far end of the bar. I headed straight to the bathroom, feeling the gaze of the bar's patrons as I passed.

I shut the door and locked it behind me.

I just murdered two men.

I washed my hands, splashed some water on my face to clean the blood off, and stared at my reflection in the graffiti-etched mirror. I was looking at a murderer. What had my life become? All of this madness because I took $20,000 from some Russian asshole? I grinned like a madman at myself—at the ridiculousness of what I was wrapped up in—snorted out a laugh, and headed back to the bar.

I ordered a double Scotch, drank it in a single gulp, and then decided to get the fuck out of there.

"Have a good one," I said to the bouncer and headed back to my loft. How could I live like this? I'd just killed two men. I was shocked at how dead I felt inside. I felt a twinge of remorse, but mostly I felt exhilarated by what had occurred. What was I becoming?

On my way home, I passed a liquor store and figured I could use some more booze to calm my nerves. I didn't think I could handle any more hallucinations from the IPA after what I'd just done.

I walked to the liquor store's Scotch section, feeling kind of fancy. I usually just went with a bottle of Cutty Sark, but tonight, in honor of my first foray into murder, I figured I'd help myself to the top shelf. I grabbed a bottle of Talisker and brought it to the counter. A black-haired woman eyed me dully. I smiled, having forgotten the rotten state of affairs my face had become.

"You alright, boss?" she asked in a thick New Jersey accent, about as thick as the makeup plastered on her face. I feared any sudden movements from her could cause an avalanche.

"Hasn't been my week," I said, and winced in pain. She looked at me skeptically. I paid her and got back some change.

"Stay out of trouble, handsome," she said.

"I'm trying," I said.

I continued home, hoping I was done with murder for the night.

23

In the morning, my head felt like a ten-ton lump of meat in the sun that burned brightly through my windows. I couldn't even feel guilt about the murders since I felt so much like death myself. I felt ground down into mush, and I didn't want to be involved with any of this shit anymore.

I looked around my studio and saw that a layer of dust had formed over all art supplies. I'd been too distracted by all the bullshit in my life to paint lately. I wondered if the CIA had some art handlers they could send to spruce up my studio and wrap up the work that was headed to Pat Hearn Gallery in the next few weeks. I had to remember to ask the next spook I saw about that. I was restless so I decided to get out of my apartment.

Great Jones was sleepy as ever, just a few burnouts dragging their drunken or hungover feet down the street toward a dumpster fire in an empty lot a few doors down.

As I walked down Broadway, every person I passed stared at my battered face. I wondered where these prying eyes had been while I was being dragged around by all these Russian hooligans the last few weeks. I felt incredibly paranoid—maybe these strangers knew I was a murderer and that was why their intrusive gazes bothered me—but tried to ignore my anxieties. I felt a deep pain on my puffy face with every footstep forward, with every strand of my hair that brushed against it, with every breeze that periodically picked up and hurled madly down the streets, as an agony screamed out for recognition for what I'd endured.

When I had first met Martin, I was an eager man full of hope and ambition for the future I intended to create for myself. I believed I held my destiny in my hands like a ball of possibility I could mold to my whims. But that was all gone. There was now just a vacancy of emotion where hope once lived. Nothing I did mattered. There were no risks. My future as the next Jeff Koons was solidified. All I had to do was to keep spooking and the life I once thought I wanted would be mine.

I walked to the mouth of the Brooklyn Bridge and climbed the slope heading toward Brooklyn. There were joggers, cyclists, skateboarders, rollerbladers, tourists, freaks, squares, and every human imaginable strolling along the bridge. Traffic skated by smoothly, and I meandered to the spot where Jacques and his men had dangled me off the bridge. I stood there gazing at the water between Manhattan and Brooklyn. Here I was, alive, breathing in the memories of my hopeless fate. I had killed two men. I felt an immense abyss welling up inside of me. No remorse. No fear. No anxiety. Just my blood as it pumped through my body and a dull pain nagging at me.

I thought of Martin, and still couldn't understand how he could be involved in all of this. I thought of his body floating like a drunken boat in the cold water below. He had had everything I could've ever wanted in his career. I wanted to jetset around the world with no concern for my bank account. I wanted dealers and collectors to fawn over me and my work. I wanted to have shows all over the world. I wanted other artists to respect me, look up to my vision. But all of these desires were nothing more than an illusion. It felt like my naivete had died with Martin.

The art world as I'd come to know it was nothing more than a scam. Every artist wanted some version of what I craved. Unfortunately, too many hopeless losers would spend their lives searching for an oasis of respectability they would never find. Nothing could save them from their lives of hopeless poverty, nothing except rich parents and a trust fund, or federal employment with the CIA.

I had killed two men.

And I'd probably kill some more.

That's what I'd become, a murderer. Where was the art in that?

I heard the sound of a family walking along the bridge. A child, maybe five years old, stopped behind me. "Why's his coat so long?" he asked his parents. I smiled at the inquisitive child.

"Because I'm a spy, kid, a secret agent." I said, doing the best Humphrey Bogart impression I could muster. They ignored me and my attempt at a transatlantic accent. I probably should've been honest, told the kid I was a fucking murderer, and could dress however the fuck I wanted.

Thursday evening rolled around and I was still stuck in a deadly mood. Frightful sounds ricocheted off the walls of my building. Shadows haunted me. Trucks barreling down Great Jones roared apocalyptic melodies. Everything felt tainted and corrupted by a new reality.

Nothing brought me any joy except drinking IPA. The bottle had been glued to my lips since the murders, and I sucked at it with a fury I'd never experienced before. My taste buds craved the intensity of the IPA, the warm rush, the glow of everything when I was fucked up. The demon detective—or Rimbaud's ghost or whatever he was—was a permanent presence in my loft. He silently floated around watching me, and I spoke to him while holding the bottle like Hamlet holding a skull, raving the soliloquies of a deranged and disordered mind, pontificating on my predicament and fate. I'd gotten used to him. He was always a welcomed guest in my hallucinations. I felt at ease when he was around; I needed him and his silent presence.

I began to crave something more, something to give my drunkenness depth. I wondered if the Toms or Agent Carol had a CIA weed connection. I bet they had some powerful, dank weed at the artist studio complex. I'd have to ask the next spook I saw about a CIA weed hookup. I'd add that to my list of questions for my new employers.

Around 9 pm my buzzer rang, and I figured it was Agent Carol here to discuss Operation MoMA. I still had difficulty imagining that the IPA could brainwash a whole mass of creative types into becoming agents of chaos directed at the mighty United States. How fucking stupid and improbable did that sound?

I opened up my window, and yelled to Agent Carol that I'd be down in a minute. I didn't want to drink more IPA in front of my partner, but I needed something to drink. The bottle of Scotch sang out to me and I grabbed it and took a giant gulp. The fragrant Scotch stopped in my throat too long and I coughed up a bunch of stomach acid and Scotch onto the floor. Shit. I got a towel and wiped it up, but the smell of sour vomit and smoky Scotch still hovered in the air. At least I wasn't trying to woo Agent Carol. One whiff of that shit and she'd be out the door in a flash.

"Oof!" she said as she walked into my loft. "Did a drunk just die in here?"

"Not yet," I said. "Sorry, I had an incident with some Scotch. It's still pretty fresh."

"We've got a pretty important mission tomorrow," she said. "You might want to dry out a bit so you're prepared for whatever comes your way. Things could get hectic with Jacques."

"Yeah, no shit!" I said. "I killed two of Jacques' men a few nights ago. I was drunk as shit, tripping on LSD, and all wavy from the Laudanum. I think I'll be fine."

"I heard about that," she said. "The first kill is the hardest to deal with. Are you doing alright?"

I didn't know how I was doing. "I'm still processing it," I said. "Not something I want to get too used to."

"You'll get over it. Soon enough it will be like second nature, sort of like going on autopilot. You won't think much about it." Her stare wasn't very reassuring. Murder wasn't something I wanted to feel indifferent to, although all I felt was dead inside.

Agent Carol was dressed in a khaki trench coat that was similar to mine, a canary yellow dress, and black Chuck Taylors smeared with the grime of Manhattan's streets. I realized I was staring at her with my mouth slightly agape, and I felt like an idiot for being so attracted to her still. She looked back at me with aloof detachment. Knowing our camaraderie was manipulated by CIA forces made me feel exploited. Our friendship had been a mirage. We shared no fraternity of the spirit. She was a spook, and I was an artist loser. Although, now I was a spook as well.

I grabbed a pack of cigarettes and the bottle of Scotch, and brought them to my coffee table.

"You want a drink while we talk about the mission?" I asked.

"No, we need to get straight to business," she said. "Besides, I can already tell you drank enough for the both of us." She seemed to lighten up a bit. Maybe we'd bond more on our mission and our fake friendship would blossom into a real one.

We could have shows all over the world as we did our CIA dirty work. It'd be fun. As I caught her glance while I poured myself some Scotch, I knew it'd never work out that way. Hope had become a completely foreign feeling to me.

"Tomorrow night should go pretty smoothly," she said. "Dmitry Vaga's pop-up was set up by Jacques and one of our collectors, a friend of the organization. We'll head there together, go to the after party, and try to convince Jacques to come back here to your place."

"But if Jacques is this KGB thug, won't he have an inkling that we're involved with the CIA? I killed two of his men. He has to know, or at least be suspicious of me by now."

"If Jacques had any idea you're with us, you'd be dead," she said. "He would've thrown you off that bridge. We're certain he wasn't trying to kill you the other night. He was just trying to scare you. You're the one that escalated the situation. Besides, I've been seeing Jacques, working undercover for the mission, and I think he actually likes you. He likes your work and thinks it's very weird and interesting. Or at least he likes torturing you." I felt jealous instantly.

"Seeing Jacques?" I asked. "In what sense?"

"He thinks we're dating," Agent Carol said. I felt angry but quickly remembered I had to abandon my unrequited love for Elena. The person I thought I knew was a fictional character, and whatever feelings I had for her were misguided and absurd. But it still burned me up inside to imagine Jacques and Elena having a romantic fling.

"How are we gonna convince him to come back here?" I asked.

Agent Carol reached into her trench coat and pulled out a gallon bag of cocaine, shaking it in her fist. "He's got one fatal flaw. He's addicted to this. We believe his addiction is the reason he's so deeply involved with the KGB and FSB. After his career crashed in Russia, he got involved in the international drug trade. The BND began gathering intelligence concerning Jacques' drug smuggling. He made tons of contacts in the arts all over Europe buying and selling large shipments of drugs and contraband. He got caught in West Germany smuggling heroin, cocaine, and barbiturates with Rainer Werner Fassbinder."

"The king of New German Cinema?" I asked in shock.

"Yes, that's him," she said. "Fassbinder finagled a deal with the authorities to get Jacques out of prison. Together they ran the underworld in West Germany, but they had some sort of falling out. Many think it was a lover's quarrel although details are sketchy and unsubstantiated. It's known in international, cultural espionage circles that Jacques spiked Fassbinder's cocktail, resulting in his overdose and death."

"Damn," I said. "I love his movies. Fuck Jacques if he killed him."

"You'll have half an eighth of cocaine stashed in this necklace." She pulled out a golden necklace with what looked like a bullet pendant dangling from the chain. She unscrewed the top, pulled out a little spoon, brought it to her nose, and sniffed, wiggling her nose. "It's really good coke. Pure uncut Peruvian cocaine. Here, do a bump."

I was shocked because I'd never seen Elena–or Agent Carol–do coke before, but I did a bump and then another in the other nostril. The minty cocaine slid down my nasal cavity, leaving me numb and buzzed. I was immediately energized. I felt my eyes turn into tiny needle points. I stood up and smoothed my hair back with my sweaty palms and felt like I had to take a shit.

"Holy fuck, this is really good!" I said. "Are you going to leave that whole bag here tonight?"

"God, no. Not with that response. You'll never get coke this pure in New York."

"The Toms also said Jacques has more IPA, and might want

me to store it here," I said. "Is that still part of the plan?"

"Yes, we think that might be another reason he might want to come back here as well," she said. "But we have another new recruit with a studio that he might want to use. The cocaine is just another carrot to dangle in front of him."

"You really think some coke is enough to get Jacques back here?" I asked. "Isn't he already pretty suspicious of me? I mean, he keeps sending his goons to fuck with me. He wants to silence me, and he certainly has to know I killed his men. And can't he get coke anywhere in New York? I mean, I could go to Max Fish right now and get coke if I asked around. Why would he come back to my place now, after all of this, just to do some blow?"

"That's true, but this isn't the regular, shitty coke you could get at Max Fish," she said. "This is one hundred percent pure cocaine. It hasn't been cut with anything. Jacques will do anything for pure Peruvian cocaine. The DEA raided a shipment of over a ton of coke and about as much heroin. The shipment was destined for Jacques' organization. He's been a fiend for pure coke since we disrupted his supply. There'll be multiple agencies watching this loft tomorrow night. We've got CIA, DEA, and FBI watching. Plus the BND will be on hand to assist. Martin had been helping the BND and CIA for two decades. We knew Martin's health was in decline, but we didn't know he had liver cancer. He had been dangerously drunk for so long, but his death was a wake up call to neutralize Jacques."

I didn't want to think about Martin. His death was always in the back of my mind. I just wanted the mission to be done with. I didn't care about all this international spy bullshit. I didn't want to kill anyone else. Even if it could save democracy in the United States. I still didn't give a shit about that.

"Anything else you need to brief me on?" I asked.

"I'll meet you here at 7 pm tomorrow and we can catch a cab

to Dmitry's show together," Agent Carol said. She took out the giant bag of cocaine, dropping a little mound of powder on the table. "Here's a little parting gift. Don't stay up too late tonight."

I smiled. "That reminds me, can the CIA get me some weed?" I asked. "I want to stop drinking so much and start smoking a lot of pot instead."

"What do you think we are, a bunch of drug dealers?" she asked.

"Uh, yeah, I do. You just walked in here with a giant bag of cocaine. I don't think I need to tell you about all the shitty drug dealing the agency is responsible for."

"We can work something out for you if we successfully apprehend Jacques and sabotage Operation MoMA," Agent Carol said, standing up. "But it's all wholly contingent on completing the mission."

24

As we approached the show, I saw a large crowd of people hanging outside the opening. It looked like a packed house. We got out of the cab and I told Agent Carol I'd meet her inside. I wanted to smoke a cigarette and hit the flask of IPA before I subjected myself to Dmitry Vaga's show.

I didn't recognize any of the chain-smokers hanging outside, as I joined them to inhale some death in preparation for what was to come. I felt like an unwanted interloper smoking with the crowd. I stomped out my cigarette, took another chug from the flask, and walked through the crowded doorway. Inside were curios objects Dmitry had bought from a shop upstate and brought here as his show. Each antique piece had a Chanel logo silkscreened on it. Many of the logos were subtle and required a brief investigation to find. Jesus fucking Christ, that was the show.

The dim lighting of the room created an ambiance of intrigue and exclusivity. It smelled like an old rich lady and the air was stuffy and hot compared to the cool evening I'd just stepped in from. Chatter softly swelled as I took stock of the crowd, most of whom were old folks who'd descended from their Upper East Side mansions to get a bit of culture. Hushed conversations floated about the room, giving the curios a weight of precious silence. I heard an old woman hailing Dmitry Vaga as a genius. He was so talented, zany, blah, blah. I couldn't be sure if it was the Chanel No. 5 coursing through the air or the rot I felt in my soul that made me want to vomit.

It struck me as insane that a man who didn't ever have to lift a finger to live a charmed life would choose to dedicate his life to pretending to be an artist. Of course the show would sell out. And, of course he didn't need the money. Maybe I was just an asshole. I guessed it was possible for Dmitry to make art for art's sake. I was just as guilty of seeking money and fame. The only difference was I had to make money to live, and I resented the fact that Dmitry didn't. I thought about Dmitry's friendship with Jacques, and how he was able to associate freely with a murderous criminal without fear of anyone, or any agency, fucking with him. My blood began to boil. If I had any reservations about killing Jacques, they'd all vanished into a red rage as this bullshit show overtook my thoughts.

I spotted Agent Carol talking with her dealer and a few collectors in a corner. In the opposite corner of the room, I saw Jacques' Gesualdo-looking ass talking to Dmitry as loving admirers surrounded them. It seemed like Jacques had shown up alone tonight. Nobody in the room looked like they could be his henchmen, or looked like they didn't belong. Other than a few easy to spot artists, the crowd was mainly old, wealthy elites.

Dmitry was wearing a red cashmere turtleneck with a Chanel logo stitched onto the bicep of the right sleeve, matching red leather pants, and white leather Beatle boots. I assumed he was wearing Chanel from head to toe; and he looked like a fucking dumbass. Jacques was dressed in a black velvet tuxedo that was fitted perfectly to his thin body. His curly black mop was gelled back and glistened like wet worms. They both looked very dapper, very chic, and very ready to fucking die.

I made my way over to Agent Carol and tried to join her conversation, but mainly just awkwardly stood behind her shoulder as my mind raced thinking of the mission. I cleared my throat and her dealer gave me a disgusted look as she swiftly exited the conversation.

"Agent Carol," I whispered. "What's the deal? Everything good?"

"It's Elena," she said through clenched teeth. "Are you a fucking idiot?"

"Oops, my bad," I said. "Dmitry and Jacques are over there." I nodded my head in their direction.

"Yeah, I have fucking eyes." She was right. She had eyes, just not for me and my smooth spy tactics. "I'm going to head over there, try to get Jacques to come back to your place. Give me a few minutes with him, then come up and offer him a bump. Then we'll convince him to come back to your place to do more coke."

Agent Carol headed over to the men, and I stepped outside for a smoke and more of Kippenberger's IPA. I lit one up, and chugged from the flask to let the psychedelic relaxation commence. I took the necklace out and did a bump in each nostril. After a few more drags, gulps, and bumps, I was ready to get this shit done.

I headed back into the show and sure enough, Agent Carol had Jacques wrapped around her finger. It looked like things were going according to plan as Agent Carol cooed flirtatiously into Jacques' ear. I felt jealous seeing Agent Carol with Jacques, but I knew I had to let the anger go. It was just part of the mission, and Agent Carol was just doing her job, and doing it very well. I pretended to nonchalantly meander over to them in a circuitous route, trying to look casual and lost in thought as I ground my teeth anxiously.

The cocaine had me feeling both energized and numb. Just beyond Agent Carol and Jacques, I could see Dmitry was surrounded by a circle of loving sycophants. Meanwhile, Agent Carol was really working her magic on Jacques. I guessed being a charming and beautiful woman was a pretty good way to lure a cokehead to his death.

"What's up?" I said as I approached, my introduction as smooth as a record scratch. Agent Carol and Jacques both glared at me.

"Always a pleasure to see you, Johnny," Jacques said, his tone mocking.

"Johnny," Agent Carol said, "you have any more of that stuff? It was really good."

"Oh, uh, yeah, I do," I said and pulled the necklace out of my pocket. "A collector of mine has some Peruvian connection or something."

I passed the necklace to Agent Carol so she could do a bump. She then passed it to Jacques. He took a few bumps, and then leaned his head back to let the cocaine drip from his sinuses into his lanky KGB body. In that moment, I couldn't help but imagine Jacques and Agent Carol having blissful, steamy sex atop a giant mountain of cocaine.

"Fuck, this is some some serious shit. You said a collector gave this to you?" Jacques asked with a tinge of suspicion in his voice. I couldn't believe he was speaking so civilly to me. He had to know I'd killed his men. So why was he being so friendly?

"Yeah, he traded me an ounce for a painting I made that I didn't even like," I said. I pretended to be ecstatic. "I don't have much left in here, but I've got a lot more of it back at my loft. Maybe we could stop there before we hit up the after party."

"I could use a pick-me-up before these people bore me to death at the after party," Jacques said. "I hate these stupid fucking openings." So did I. Jacques and I were so alike.

"I'm in," Agent Carol said. We caught each other's eye. I couldn't believe this stupid little plan was working. Who'd have thought the best way to ensnare a man wanted for conspiracy, murder, and terrorism was a little bit of cocaine?

The show was dying down, and the art world elites prepared to party on at the next destination. I heard lots of dumbasses congratulating Dmitry as they left. The fear I felt at the beginning of the night had begun to creep back into my nerves. Agent Carol and I had never talked about what would happen once we lured Jacques back to my place. Was I expected to be the killer? I guessed I had it in me. All I had to do was think of Dmitry's terrible show or Jacques and Agent Carol fucking like rabbits and my rage would fuel the murder.

"You all want to get a cab back to my place?" I asked.

"If you've got more of that shit waiting," Jacques said with a grin.

"Yeah, let's go!" Agent Carol said.

With that, we headed for the door, but of course it took Jacques a while to schmooze as he said his goodbyes. My hands began to sweat with anticipation, and I saw the demon detective in the corner of the room. He was taking in the curios, so I knew I was tripping off the IPA, but I felt good from my cocktail of illicit substances. The demon detective was a nice distraction from what was to come. I wondered if he'd owned any of these ancient objects in his previous life. I could imagine him as some eccentric genius in the seventeenth century, working diligently to carve a magnificent cabinet of curiosities. I hoped he wouldn't have put any shitty Chanel logos on them, but I doubted he would've.

Outside, Jacques, Agent Carol, and I piled into a taxi and headed toward Great Jones Street and our destiny.

25

I rolled down the window as we cruised down Park Avenue. I could smell Magnolia blossoms blooming in the evening air. Jacques sat in the middle seat necking with Agent Carol. I could hear the subtle smacking of their lips and felt sick to my stomach. I didn't want to hear them making out anymore and began getting antsy to do some more cocaine. I couldn't believe I was stuck in a cab with a fucking terrorist making out with the woman of my dreams. I took a deep breath hoping to squash the wrath I felt burning inside. I tried to picture perfectly arranged lines of coke laid out on my coffee table, fantasizing about the numb elation of dopamine that would soon flood my brain. I had to kill Jacques, but the dread I had felt about it dissipated as I looked over and saw Jacques' hand massaging Agent Carol's breast.

The taxi danced around Midtown, weaving chaotically toward the Bowery. We turned down Great Jones and I saw my favorite place in the world come into view. The taxi pulled to a stop in front of my place and I paid the man, taking a receipt so I could write off the ride as a business expense. Jacques had his arm around Agent Carol's shoulder, and the two were laughing like teenage love birds. Agent Carol made eye contact with me and I saw murder hovering deep in her stare.

We walked up the stairs, and I opened the door to my studio. My place sparkled with cleanliness and the air smelled like lemon-scented cleaning supplies. I hadn't cleaned in weeks, so I knew the CIA had sent over some agents to spruce up the loft.

"Holy shit," Jacques said. "This place is so much bigger without all the crates in it." He laughed as he took a look around, scrutinizing the paintings along my studio wall before plopping down on the couch next to Agent Carol. When I looked at Jacques sitting on my couch, the feeling of dread returned, my hands growing cold and clammy and beginning to shake. I needed to be doing something, so I fumbled with some CDs near my stereo and then pressed play. Gesualdo's arias sounded in the air as Jacques and Agent Carol began making out on my couch.

"What the fuck is this creepy music?" Jacques said as he tore himself from Agent Carol's lips.

"It's Carlo Gesualdo," I said. "He was an Italian composer from the 16th century. Ever seen his portrait? You look a lot like him. Here, hold on." I walked to my bedside, took the tacked-up photocopied portrait off the wall, and showed it to Jacques. I knew I was stalling. Fear bubbled up in my chest as my blood pressure rose, my battered face flooding red with IPA and terror. I began to feel very drunk and wanted to get more drunk, but I knew I had to get it together to do what needed to be done.

"I don't see it," Jacques said. He held the portrait for Agent Carol to see.

"Me neither," Agent Carol said. Jacques placed the portrait

on the coffee table.

I didn't want to keep dragging it out, but I wasn't sure how to proceed. "Anybody want a drink? I've got some good Scotch." I didn't really care if anyone else wanted any, but I knew I needed some to work up the nerve to kill Jacques.

"That sounds nice," Agent Carol said. She and Jacques continued to flirt on the couch as I went to the kitchen, grabbed three glasses, and set them on the table. I walked to the cupboard and found a fresh bottle of Talisker before grabbing my knife from my trench coat. I could still hear the sounds of Jacques and Agent Carol kissing on the couch. I looked at their backs from the kitchen, and saw Jacques' hand move to Agent Carol's crotch. Fuck, I was disgusted. I was outraged. I just wanted to be done with it all. I held the knife in my right hand, clicked the switchblade open, the sound masked by the smacking of their lips. The knife's steel blade transfixed me, as I brought it up to my eyes and stared deep into the steel. I brought the blade to my side and tried to psych myself up to murder the Gesualdo asshole. Fuck Jacques. Fuck CIA. Fuck Agent Carol, and fuck my misguided feelings for her.

"What the fuck's taking so long over there?" Jacques said. "Where's the blow? Where's the Scotch?"

"Sorry, man," I said. "I zoned out a bit over here. I'm kind of fucked up."

"It's all good, Johnny," Jacques said. "I just like fucking with you, but hurry up."

"Don't I know it," I said, feeling beads of cold sweat gathering on my forehead. My hands continued trembling with anticipation. They turned cold as they dampened. My armpits started to leak like a faucet, and I could smell a dank musk coming from them. My stomach ached with anxiety as I felt a million hornets flying around in it with a fury. I just had to do it. I couldn't hesitate.

I stood behind Jacques with the bottle in my left hand and the switchblade hidden behind my back in my right hand. Agent Carol and Jacques were ignoring me, lost in their little affections. I lowered the bottle over Jacques' left shoulder and interrupted their ogling, holding it near his head for him to see.

"Ever had this Scotch?" I asked. He took the bottle from my hand and brought it in front of his face to read the label.

As Jacques studied the bottle, I reached the knife over his right shoulder, and slit his throat. His head fell back as he dropped the bottle of Talisker to the floor. He looked up at me, gasping for air as blood spurted out of his neck and then fell face first onto the coffee table, his hand hitting Gesualdo's portrait that was still lying there, and causing the portrait to flutter in the air as he crashed into the rug. His lifeless eyes stared into an abyss unknown to the living. The vacant gaze cast beyond the earthly realm.

Agent Carol looked up at me. "You could've at least waited until we did a few lines!"

Before I could answer, the door burst open as agents from CIA, DEA, FBI, BND, and NYPD came rushing in surrounding us.

I dropped the knife. Several agents came over and said things to me, but nothing registered. I needed to lay down. I walked to my bed as commotion overcame my loft. Agents searched every square inch of my studio. I wasn't sure what they were looking for, but I kept an eye out because I didn't want them to take my IPA or the bottle of Talisker as evidence. More people came up to me and said things, but I couldn't understand a word that was said. All I heard was a vague static coming off the edges of things. The trauma put me into a trance. I eventually rocked softly back and forth in the fetal position, trying to erase the image of Jacques' dying breaths from my mind. Then I realized my bloody hands had dried stuck to my comforter.

That somehow snapped me out of my state of shock.

"You did good, Agent Dabs," Agent Sandal said, congratulating me before wandering away to join the other agents who were popping bottles of champagne and giving each other high fives and hugs to celebrate their victory.

A man in an FBI uniform came up to me, and put his hand out to shake mine. "Congratulations, Agent Dabs," he said as he shook my bloody hand. "We've been watching you. We're big fans of your work."

I was stunned that my artistic reputation preceded me amongst these men representing the various agencies. Then it dawned on me he wasn't talking about my artwork, but my work as an agent of international espionage. A serial killer with the CIA protecting me from being held accountable for my deeds.

"Three slit throats in less than a week," he said, beaming down at me. "That might be a new record. Keep it up and you'll have a bright career ahead of you."

I did my best to pretend that murdering Jacques didn't bother me. I got up out of bed and opened a fresh bottle of Scotch, trying to keep up with the celebratory air that had taken over my loft. Eventually, Jacques' corpse was put into a body bag to be taken to Langley for a date with the agency's coroner.

I walked back to my bed and sat drinking the Talisker straight out of the bottle, watching as the proceedings of the night came to a close. I felt dead inside, felt like a patsy, felt like a killer. Everything felt bleak, like the insanity would never end. I wondered what would be expected of me after this mission and realized I couldn't handle the pressure of being an agent of cultural espionage. I was just an artist on the make, trying to live my life in a way that solidified the ideals I held so dearly. None of that had anything to do with being associated with an organization that personified evil in my mind. Now, I was inextricably tied to that evil for the rest of my days.

Agent Carol was the last person to leave the loft. She came to bid me farewell.

"You did great tonight, Johnny."

"Uh, yeah, thanks for working with me," I said. I was ready for her to leave. I just wanted to be alone.

She reached out, grabbed my shoulder, and squeezed it affectionately. "You'll get over whatever you're feeling right now," she said. "My first mission was a mind fuck. I was inconsolable for weeks. It's totally normal to feel overwhelmed and depressed."

"Thanks, Agent Carol." I paused, trying to find some words that would articulate my confusion. "I definitely feel pretty fucked up. I don't know, I just feel like I want to sleep away this bad dream."

"You know when you have a solo show? You've put all of your energy toward making the work, promoting it, and then the show is over. The opening's over. All the excitement is gone and you just feel exhausted and depressed. The post-show blues? You're going to have that same feeling about this mission. It'll pass though. You've just got to find the next project to sink yourself into."

"Yeah, I know that feeling. Agent Carol?"

"Yes?"

"How do you live like this?"

"What do you mean?"

"How do you go from being an artist to this? An agent of this farce?"

"Honestly?" she said and chuckled. "We're paid very well. And the benefits are amazing—health insurance, a 401k. After years of struggling as an artist in this city, having any semblance of financial stability is enough for any artist to cross over to our side. I wouldn't go back even if I could."

I laughed and thought about how I'd lived in near poverty and supposed authenticity my whole life until I was recruited. "I do look forward to having health care."

With that, I stood and gave Agent Carol a hug. I walked her out of my loft and lit a cigarette as I watched her walk off toward the Bowery into the dark, lonely night.

26

The next few weeks were rough. I kept hitting the bottle of IPA with an abandon I'd never imagined was possible. I only left my apartment to find food. The thought of being surrounded by people gave me gooseflesh. The demon detective had been permanently drifting along with me everywhere I went. His silence was a solace, and I appreciated that he didn't expect anything from me. I could confide in him, and I continued my manic soliloquies as he floated around my loft, always a patient listener. Of course, I knew he was a hallucination, but he was such a comfort in the depths of the lowest point of my life. I felt protected by him and knew I was safe from harm when he was around. I thought he was like my guardian angel, but of the demon realm.

I wasn't sleeping much. My hands shook incessantly. When I woke up in the morning and forced myself out of bed, I went straight for the bottle of IPA. I wanted to erase my memories and to erase myself in the process. Meanwhile, Martin's self-portrait stared at me from the wall where I had hung it. There wasn't a better illustration for the terror I felt in the depths of my soul.

One day, I tried to get back into the groove of painting again. I gathered my brushes, squirted paint onto a palette, and attempted to paint another series of images depicting the demon detective's underworld. I tried painting the background for about ten minutes, but I just wasn't enjoying it. A feeling of ennui dragged me back to bed. My studio practice had been the focus of my life before I'd gotten involved with the CIA, but now it had turned into a horrible reminder of the reality I inhabited. I felt shackled to this fate, trapped in a life I didn't want to live. Whenever I held a pencil, pen, or paintbrush in hand, I thought of the countless hours I'd spent in all the shitty rooms I'd made art in since I'd moved to New York almost a decade before. Back then, my ambition had ignited a spark in me to persevere. I'd always had the feeling that this batch of paintings, or the next, would be the one that opened up a world of success, and laid an abundance of possibilities at my feet. But now I knew better. The world was there at my fingertips, and every success imaginable was within my grasp—and my role as a CIA agent clinched this fact. Because of this, everything felt empty. I knew at some point, Agent Carol would be correct in her assertion that these feelings would pass. But that didn't assuage any of the guilt I felt.

What was the point of growing as an artist when nothing I made actually mattered? I couldn't continue working for the CIA as an agent of cultural espionage. I wanted to be a creative, free spirit, but that reality was impossible. Only the independently wealthy like Dmitry Vaga could live like that. I was a casualty to my own less prosperous roots.

Eventually, after maybe days or maybe weeks had passed—I

was too fucking drunk to keep track—the sound of my buzzer snapped me out of my tortured head space. I went to my window and saw Eduardo on my stoop.

Fucking great, just what I wanted, a surprise visit and reminder of what awaited me. I opened the window and signaled I'd be down to retrieve him. I knew he was here to discuss the show at Pat Hearn, but I couldn't even feign excitement. It was the big break I had always hoped for, but under the entirely wrong circumstances.

"How have you been?" Eduardo asked as I grabbed a bottle of Scotch and two glasses.

"I've been alright. Just trying to wrap my head around the last few months."

I handed Eduardo a glass of Scotch.

"None for me. It's too early," Eduardo said as he raised his hand to deny my offering. I didn't mind drinking his portion. "You look pretty sick," he said. I just stared, waiting for him to get on with it. "Everything's settled with Pat Hearn. We got your work from Langley yesterday. The show looks great and Pat's really excited to work with you."

"My work from Langley?" I was surprised. I'd forgotten the CIA studios were now cranking out my work. "Oh, right, Langley. Cool, I guess that's it, right?" I wanted to get the show out of the way, and I wanted to get Eduardo out of my apartment.

Eduardo looked at me skeptically. "You haven't checked out your studio in Langley?" he asked. "It's pretty state of the art. You'll be jealous you don't have access to their resources in the city."

I caught a whiff of my stench as I raised the glass of Scotch to my mouth. I hadn't showered in a few days and had been wearing the same clothes for a week. "Yeah, haven't made it down there yet. I don't really know what to do with myself these days."

"Don't beat yourself up. It takes a while to get used to all of this."

I sat there silently, but remembered a question that had been plaguing me. "Eduardo?"

"What's up?"

"Did you write your novel?" I asked. I really wanted to know. I'd looked up to him so much when I read his book.

"That little thing?" Eduardo said. "Of course not. I'm not much of a writer. The CIA has a very prolific wing of ghostwriters. Every book you see at a bookstore put out by a major publishing house was more than likely written in Langley at the arts complex."

It surprised me how devastated I was by the revelation. I felt bad for whoever wrote Eduardo's book. I also felt bad for whoever was making my work for me. Everything I once held dear was a fucking joke. What a fool I was to believe art mattered at all.

"Everything's settled then?" I asked, ready to be alone to bask in my despair.

"Everything's good to go." Eduardo forced a smile. I knew he was eager to get the fuck out of my loft that surely smelled like a mixture of a Scotch distillery and death. "The opening's this Thursday. Pat can't wait to see you." The demon detective hovered behind Eduardo as he rose to leave.

A few days later I went to the opening at Pat Hearn. The CIA artists had made some really great Johnny Dabs paintings—much better than anything I would've made. There were five square canvases on the gallery wall, each about four feet by four feet. The colors were DayGlo bright and depicted psychedelic images of beer bottles exploding, the letters IPA written in bubble letters and erupting all over the canvas, and numerous little beer or garden gnomes with angel wings holding beer steins flying out of the wreckage. The beer bottles shattered across the canvas, and they were funny as shit. Were my new CIA assistants fucking with me? It felt like a cruel joke, but I was the star of the show. A few months ago I would've felt ecstatic, like I was the king of the art scene. But now I felt completely bored and alienated by the scene

"Dude," D'Angelo said as we stood in the center of the gallery watching the art scenesters enjoying my paintings. "Such a sick show. These paintings are far out and such a strange new direction for you. These aren't what I was expecting." He patted me on the back.

"Thanks, man," I said. "Are you involved with the organization?" I realized I had forgotten to ask Agent Carol whether our mutual friend was also federally employed.

D'Angelo looked around the room. "Can't talk about that right now, man," he said. "Maybe we can get a drink in Langley soon." He winked at me.

"Have you heard from Elena?" I asked. "I figured she'd be here." A group of four artists I sort of knew approached us.

"She couldn't make it," D'Angelo said. "She told me to send you her best. Congrats again, Johnny. Let's get that drink soon." I felt disappointed. He left me as the artists took turns shaking my hand, reintroducing themselves, and congratulating me on the show.

My reputation as an important emerging artist had been solidified, and all my former art world dreams had become reality. Fame and fortune were mine, but I felt worse than I ever had before. I kept telling myself to enjoy it, but I couldn't, not under these circumstances.

I didn't even go to the after party at Pat Hearn's apartment. I made up an excuse, gave Pat a kiss on the cheek, and walked home from Alphabet City, prepared for danger like the paranoiac I'd become. I hadn't gone out at night since I'd murdered

Jacques, considering that all of my night wanderings had led to death recently. But I welcomed the possibility that night. I was ready to kill–and just as ready to die. The thought scared the shit out of me.

After the night of the opening, I decided to lay off the IPA for a while. I quit cold turkey. The worst part was coming off the Laudanum. I was burning up, then felt like I was freezing to death. My hands shook with delirium tremens. And I had waking nightmares, visions far more sinister than anything I'd seen while tripping on the IPA. The demon detective had disappeared, and had been replaced by an old naked man who stood in the corner of my loft silently screaming. He alternated between scratching his body with his fingernails until he bled and hitting his head against the wall. He made me miss the demon detective.

After a week of feeling like I had the flu, the withdrawal symptoms finally disappeared and I slowly emerged from my depression. My face had healed, but I now had a small scar on my cheek that I knew would always remind me of Jacques. A new hope had begun to scrub the drunken cobwebs from my mind. I went to the bank to check my balance and found I had exactly $100,000 in my account. I figured the rate was $33,333.33 per person murdered. I could've lived alright in New York on two assassinations a year.

A few weeks later, my buzzer rang. I looked down and saw the Toms on my stoop, Great Jones Street's hustling winos begging them for alms.

"So, what's up, boys?" I asked, as the three of us sat down inside my loft.

"We have a new mission for you," Sandal said.

"You're going to like this one," Schneider said, looking excited to unveil the new mission.

"About that new mission . . ." I began. "I can't work for the organization anymore."

The Toms smiled at me, knowing full well what my objections were. "Everyone says that, Agent Dabs!" Schneider said. "At the end of the day, you pledged yourself to the organization. This isn't a fucking job you can just quit."

"Yeah, Johnny," Sandal said. "Every agent has their doubts in the beginning. You'll get over them soon enough."

"I'd rather not. I refuse to do this next mission," I said sternly. "I'm not capable of doing this anymore. I can't just murder people willy-nilly on the organization's behalf. I don't want to devote my life to preserving American cultural hegemony. I don't give a shit what happens to art or culture anymore. Fuck all this. I want out."

The agents stared at me. I was sure they'd heard this speech a million times before. I didn't care. They could lock me up for the rest of my life. Nothing mattered anymore.

"Do you realize what you're leaving behind?" Sandal said. "This studio? It's ours. Your precious art career? We created it, and we can damn sure take it away from you. You'll never show in this city again. All your hard work, all the promise we saw in you, you want to throw that all away?"

"Throw it in the fucking garbage for all I care. I just want to get away from all of this."

"Come on, give it at least a week," Schneider said. "We've invested a lot of resources in you. It'd be a shame to see you just give up on it like that."

"My mind's made up." It felt easier than I expected. At least that's what I thought at the time. But nothing is ever easy.

"You have to have a psych evaluation before we can give you your exit papers," Sandal said. "And you have to be out of this loft by the end of the month. That's in six days."

That was that. I walked the Toms out, feeling excited to close this chapter of my life.

The next day I was summoned to a psychiatrist's office on the Upper East Side on Fifth Avenue and 88th Street, next to the Guggenheim. It was just a few blocks from Dmitry Vaga's disastrous, yet incredibly successful, pop-up show.

I sat on the psychiatrist's fainting couch while the Guggenheim mocked me from the window. The doctor ran some sort of Rorschach tests and then interviewed me for about an hour about my experiences working with the CIA. He told me I had been suffering from delusions of grandeur that sprang from a borderline narcissistic personality disorder. I couldn't argue with that. I didn't mention the hallucinogenic visions that had been haunting me for the last year.

I was all ready to leave with a clean bill of mental health when I was sent to another room for one last evaluation.

The doctor led me to a door labeled "SLEEP ROOM." Inside, I found a room almost empty of furnishings with concrete floors and white padded cell walls. A single light bulb dangled menacingly from the ceiling. In the center of the floor, I saw a drain with dark stains around it that looked like dried blood. I got the chills immediately. There was one exam chair sitting lonely in the room, just beyond the drain. The psychiatrist left as a nurse entered the room and ordered me to sit. She began strapping me into the chair. I started to resist.

"What are you doing to me?" I asked, growing agitated.

"Don't worry," she said. "It'll be over before you know it." I tried yanking my hands free but she'd already bound and secured them. She went out the door and rolled in a metal cart covered with a blue cloth, a lonely syringe in the center.

"What are you giving me?" I yelled.

"Relax, it's just insulin," she replied in a soothing voice. "A natural hormone your body produces. Nothing to worry about."

In between doses of insulin, I faded in and out of consciousness. A high-definition film was projected on the ceiling above me. The film showed every horror of war, every horror of the twentieth century: mutilated corpses piled high in mass graves, people committing genocide while smiling for the cameras, starving children and adults who looked like walking skeletons. In between these terrible visions were patriotic, postcard-like film clips of American excellence. Americana was portrayed as the saving grace amidst the horror. The whole experience felt like a bout of dementia, and left me disoriented and confused. I felt a ravenous hunger, knew something horrible was occurring but couldn't make sense or remember why I was there. I knew they were trying to erase my memory or brainwash me, to make me forget what I knew and what I'd been a part of. Eventually, I came to once they stopped giving me shots of insulin for a few hours. My mind's haze began to drift away, and I began to feel steady. I pretended the brainwashing worked by saying "Death to those evil commies!" over and over to the nurses that came to check in on me every half hour or so after the insulin shots had stopped. I feigned confusion and did my best to hide the outrage cycling through my recovering, insulin-addled mind. I just wanted to get the fuck out of there.

A nurse came in to let me know I would be released in a few hours. I had no idea how long I'd been trapped there, but after filling out some paperwork, I was free to go. They gave me a three-month supply of Lithium and an address to a storage facility in Long Island City where all my stuff had been moved. They had already cleared out my loft for the next desperate artist.

I went to the bank to check my balance again. The money in my account hadn't been touched. I wondered if they'd left me the hundred grand as a bribe to keep my mouth shut. I took out ten grand and took a train out to Long Island City.

On my way to the storage facility, I stopped at a used car lot. I figured I'd need a car if I wanted to get out of town and make my escape. I saw a used 1991 Ford Bronco, took it for a test drive, and paid for it in cash. Then I drove to the storage facility and packed up only the books, records, and Martin's artwork. I left all of my furniture and art supplies for the CIA to deal with.

I drove out of New York with no destination in mind. My bank account was still fat, and I had no financial obligations to worry about. I said goodbye to New York City, its majesty in my rearview mirror as I watched the skyline disappear into memory. I had no idea where I was going, and I didn't care. Just anywhere but there.

27

How do you start your life over from scratch? I'd just turned thirty and had no clue what I was going to do. I drove west, not knowing where I'd end up. Los Angeles was the first place I thought of, but I knew the CIA was there, their eyes watching over every act of creativity in the city. Then I thought of my hometown of Houston. It wasn't exactly a major cultural capital with a vibrant art scene, so I figured maybe the CIA didn't have a full-fledged operation there. Plus, my parents still lived there. I'd been a neglectful son over the last year, and I felt a bit guilty about that.

When I arrived in Houston, I found that all of the people I knew from the art scene were gone. Most had moved in search of greener pastures and better opportunities, just as I'd done almost a decade before. The others had dropped out of the art scene to focus on building themselves a life far away from their youthful flirtations with bohemia.

I found a job teaching at an art-centered magnet school in

the Houston school district. It turned out that being surrounded by awkward teenagers in love with making art was exactly
what I needed. I enjoyed mentoring the students. It gave me
hope for humanity to see these kids so elated and inspired by
the things they created.

After a few years of teaching, I finally found my groove with
painting and drawing again. I befriended some artists and went
to openings and bars with them. We gossiped about the scene,
just like I had done way back when in New York City. I showed
my work in Houston, Austin, and Dallas occasionally, but I
cared more about making the work than I did showing it or
trying to make sales.

I explored Houston and did my best to enjoy the ugly, oily
megalopolis. I still fancied myself a Situationist, so I continued
going on dérives, but it was usually too hot to walk around comfortably. Instead, I took long, aimless drives, trading the gridded
streets of Manhattan for the hectic freeways of Houston. My
favorite thing to do was drive around the 610 loop, listening to
Lightnin' Hopkins' blues drawl out of my speakers. As I drove
over the ship channel, I'd let poor Lightnin' comfort me. The
surrounding petrochemical plants exhaled polluted smoke into
the humid atmosphere, creating a haze over the flat landscape
that rolled on and on into the distance. Sometimes, I'd try to
be absolutely modern, letting the slowed and chopped sounds
of DJ Screw guide my vessel. Between Lightnin' Hopkins and
DJ Screw, I didn't think another sound could encapsulate the
lackadaisical cityscape anymore beautifully.

Every once in a while, I'd head out to Lawndale Forest Park
Cemetery and visit Lightnin' Hopkins's grave. The flat green
lawn of the dead gave me some perspective on life. Here we
were on this Earth, so much to do, so many possibilities before
us, and all that is waiting for us in the end is a lonely little marble slab on the ground, no matter how fucking great we were.

Sometimes I saw a fire in the eyes of my students that reminded me of myself at their age. Many would go on to good art schools after graduation, and then try to make names for themselves in New York, Chicago, Los Angeles, Berlin, or London—anywhere but Texas. I wished them luck, knowing full well the harsh reality that awaited them. A few rose to the top, and I wondered if they'd been snatched up by the CIA, but I'd never know. Certainly, they'd never tell me if they were one of the chosen ones.

My memories of life as a CIA agent faded into the back of my mind. The doctor's attempt to erase my memories hadn't worked, but I thought about that year of my life less and less frequently. New York City, and the many years I spent there chasing my dreams, now seemed nothing more than a fairy tale. It almost felt like it all had happened to another person, or that I'd shed that part of my skin long ago. For the most part, I thought very little about those last few months in New York. I didn't want to know the things I knew, didn't want to be reminded of what I'd done. The memories of the two men lying dead in the alley and of Jacques bleeding on my floor would always be with me. I just tried not to lose sleep over it.

Sometime around 2010, I was grocery shopping, and stopped in the beer aisle to grab a six pack. I'd mostly stopped drinking since my time as a CIA operative, but every once in a while, I liked to drink a few on the weekends. I stood staring at the refrigerated shelves of beer as the letters IPA burned my eyes. My memories of Kippenberger's beer flickered around my brain like a wildfire. I felt faint, and immediately broke out in a cold sweat. I couldn't believe the number of IPAs available on the shelves. Seeing those letters again, I thought of Martin Kippenberger and the IPA he'd given me so many years ago. I bought a six pack to see what it tasted like, fiending for the harsh hooch of my past.

When I got home, I put my groceries away, put on a Lightnin' Hopkins record, sat on my couch, and cracked open a beer. The bitterness flooded my palate, and I let the blues in my bottle slide down my throat. I enjoyed the way it tasted, but it was like drinking water compared to Kippenberger's beer.

After the third IPA, I stood up and looked at the painting Martin had given me, which now hung prominently above my couch. I raised my glass in a toast to Martin and chugged the rest of the beer down.

I rarely had visitors over to my place, but when I did, they always asked about Martin's painting. I usually just said that an old friend of mine from my days in New York had painted it. I still had the giant stack of Martin's hotel drawings too. I had framed his portrait of Lola and hung it up in my bedroom. The beautiful German woman, her form crystallized by Martin's desperate, drunk hand, was a memory of a life I'd lost long ago. But I cherished her memory, wondered where she was, whether she was alive and breathing.

And then there was Agent Carol, but I mostly referred to her in my thoughts as Elena. After the night I murdered Jacques, she disappeared from my life, and I never saw her in person again. She was now a legitimate art star represented by Gagosian Gallery. If I picked up an issue of *ArtForum*, I'd almost always see an advertisement for a solo show of hers in some exotic locale with one of the most powerful galleries in the art world. Considering she was a household name, I assumed she was still spooking. Many of my students loved her work, and I was always glad to bring her up in my lectures about contemporary painting. I had no hard feelings or resentment toward her. She was just doing what she needed to do. I couldn't blame her for wanting a successful career.

I had seen so much great art during my time in New York, but nothing ever inspired me the way Martin's work did. He was the real deal, and I never cared whether the CIA had made his work for him. Even if they did, it was one of the most interesting oeuvres of any artist in the final decades of the twentieth century. I watched his star continue to rise, even years after his death. His career trajectory went all the way to the heavens. I knew he deserved every iota of respect that came his way after death—even if his success was largely due to his association with the CIA and BND. His work stood on its own, even if his career was manufactured by unseen hands. I was proud to have known him and to have been chosen by him, even if our friendship had turned me into a murderer. To have known Martin Kippenberger was to know divinity itself. I would go to my grave knowing I had touched greatness in my day, now long ago, on Great Jones.

About a week ago, I ran into a former student at a coffee shop. She had moved to Los Angeles to pursue the bohemian life. I wasn't sure what she did out there, but she seemed happy to be in that beautiful city full of opportunity and promise. She said there was an art show happening that night in Houston that I couldn't miss. Evidently, this young artist was showing his work in New York to rave reviews, selling out shows, and making a go of it from Houston. She gave me the address, and with no obligations that evening, I went to see what all of the commotion was about.

The gallery was in a decrepit house just north of downtown Houston. There were kids outside, all in their mid-twenties I guessed. They looked like they'd been transported directly from a show I would've gone to in Alphabet City in the nineties. The clothes, the hairstyles, the piercings, and the clunky shoes made them look like extras from a film about my glory days in New York City.

I took in the jaded stares of the kids smoking cigarettes and

drinking beers outside the opening. I recognized their quizzi-
cal looks as my old ass walked into the gallery.

Inside, I stood in front of a painting composed of thick globs
of bright pigment that depicted a lumpy head laying on a table
with a hand coming out from under it, holding an empty bottle
that the head's eyeball stared straight into. My former student
was right. The show was phenomenal. I could feel a raw energy emanating out of the paintings on the wall. There were
also strange corporeal sculptures—three gnarly, scarred fingers
standing five-feet tall placed at random intervals in the room, a
four-feet tall left and right ear merged together dangling from
the ceiling at about eye level, a seven-feet tall nose standing on
the floor in one of the corners of the gallery's walls—large and
imposing in their scale and ambition. I was surprised by how
impressed I was, and immediately thought of Martin. Most of
the work wouldn't look out of place in a museum retrospective
of Kippenberger's work. I looked at the rest of the show and
wondered what strange creature had made this work. It made
sense this kid was on the up and up. I just hoped New York
wouldn't break him the way it broke me. I knew what he was
up against.

A young man approached me. "Uh, hello, sir," he said awkwardly. "I'm Nathan, this is my gallery." He put his hand out to
shake mine. "Let me know if you've got any questions. Here's
a price list, if you're interested." He handed me the sheet of
paper. I knew he thought I was old, and probably had some
money to throw around.

"Nice to meet you, Nathan," I said. "I'm Johnny Dabs. Is the
artist here? I really love this work. I have a question for him." I
had just one thing on my mind.

"Yeah, he's floating around here somewhere. Give me a second, I'll bring him over." He walked off in search of the artist.

Five minutes later, Nathan approached with a sheepish-looking youngster who seemed indifferent to all of the buzz at the opening. He was tall and lanky with jet black hair messed about. His forearms had small glyphs, words, and cartoony doodles tattooed on them.

"Mr, uh, Johnny," Nathan said, obviously bad at his new-found profession. "This is Jimmy, Jimmy Sunblade. This is his show."

I stuck my hand out to Jimmy Sunblade. "Hey, I really dig your show. It's great," I said with no need to fake excitement.

"Thanks, nice to meet you," he said.

"Are you familiar with the work of Martin Kippenberger?" I asked. I could tell by his blank stare that I had a story to tell him. I figured I'd just pull out my phone, show him some pictures of Martin's work instead.

Acknowledgements

I'd like to thank my first readers: Alika Herreshoff, Hayden Anderson, Sam Rowell, and Russell Etchen. Your notes were incredibly valuable, and I thank you from the bottom of my heart for taking the time to read this novel in its early stage.

I'd also like to thank my editors Allie Wuest and Jesse Coleman. I appreciate your expertise and for making this so much better than it was.

So much gratitude goes to Seth Alverson for creating such an amazing painting for the cover.

Thanks to Sebastian Forray for the design of the cover, back cover, and layout of the book.

I also would like to thank Katie Guilfoyle for all the support she offered during the first couple of drafts.

I want to shout out to Cody Ledvina for making the advertisement that I haven't seen yet, and for being an extraordinary human being and artist. You're my favorite artist of all time!

I'd like to thank Lindsay Arnold for putting me up in Ernest Hemingway's suite at the Monteleone in New Orleans while I was editing the last draft, and for the smoky author photo.

Lastly, I'd like to thank my family for putting up with the ages of indigence that I never seem able to escape.

Oh, also I should thank Martin Kippenberger for inspiring me to write this novel. Your confounding oeuvre continues to baffle me and encourages me to keep it weird with my own work.